The Meetinghouse Tragedy

The
Meetinghouse
Tragedy

❧ ❧

An Episode in the Life of a
New England Town

❧ ❧

Charles E. Clark

Including Illustrations by
John W. Hatch

University of New Hampshire
Published by University Press of New England
Hanover and London

University of New Hampshire

Published by University Press of New England

Hanover, NH 03755

© 1998 by the Trustees of the University of New Hampshire

Printed in the United States of America

5   4   3   2   1

CIP *data appear at the end of the book*

In honor of
Timothy Carlton, Simeon Fletcher, George Lancey,
Joseph Severance, and Reuben Stiles
who died in the meetinghouse tragedy

❧ ❧

and in loving memory of
Martha Evans Wright, 1864–1945
and
Beatrice Wright Clark, 1905–1996
through whose hands the Polly Lewis–Phebe Howard copy
of the ballad came to me.

Contents

❦ ❧

Illustrations

❧ ❧

FIGURE 1. *Phebe Howard Smith, to whom the author's copy of the meetinghouse ballad was given in 1779, the year of her birth. Photo from a daguerreotype in author's possession by University of New Hampshire Photographic Services.*

Preface

❧ ❧

This is a variation on the old trunk-in-the-attic theme, the often imagined but seldom realized serendipitous discovery right under one's nose of a gem that opens up a story, a piece of history. Sort of like Hawthorne's scarlet letter. In this case it was a stitched pamphlet of forty-three handwritten verses, inserted between the pages of a family Bible. In 1974 my mother handed the Bible over to me, making me its sixth documented owner. My first-born, a daughter, will be its seventh.

The pamphlet bears the maiden name, Phebe Howard, of the second wife of the Bible's first owner, and records the date, July 25, 1779, upon which it was "given to her," presumably by one whose name also appears (and whom I had wrongly assumed was the author), Polly Lewis. The year the pamphlet was given to Phebe, it turns out, was also the year of her birth.

The verses describe a terrible accident during the raising of a meetinghouse in 1773. As one whose professional interests involve the period and region of the event, I took more than a casual notice of the verses. I promised myself that some day, when the decks were cleared of other responsibilities, I would look into the event upon which the verses were based, though I believed for a long time that the episode would be of interest mainly as a small chapter in the history of a family. The verses, I thought, must have been given to Phebe because of some personal connection, though what that connection might have been was not immediately evident. It turns out there was no such personal connection at all that I can discover, other than the obvious value that Phebe attached to the possession of the manuscript.

It was twenty years after assuming the stewardship of the Bible and its contents, when I began what was still a casual investigation by seeing if I could find any contemporary newspaper accounts of the accident, that the story began to grow. Since the location of the Howard family, and the Smith family into which Phebe married, was eastern Massachusetts, I had assumed that general location to be the venue of the verses and the most likely site of the accident. But the place that is named is Wilton, and there is no Wilton, Massachusetts. A look through the files of several Boston newspapers from the autumn of 1773 disclosed that the accident had in fact occurred in Wilton, New Hampshire. As it happened, I had recently been appointed to a university chair established specifically to promote the study of that province and state. Obviously, it was time to learn more.

Eventually, as more of the pieces fell into place, the meetinghouse tragedy, as I began calling the episode, moved closer to the center of my cluster of New Hampshire-related projects. Somewhere along the line, prompted in part by the appointment of a research assistant with a background in architecture, I decided to wait no longer to try to find out all I could about the meetinghouse, though it no longer stands, and to understand its construction and the calamitous event of September 7, 1773. I wondered whether the re-creation of this dramatic episode, along with a close look at what I now recognized as quite a remarkable ballad, might perhaps add texture to our picture of Revolutionary-era rural communities and at the same time make a compelling story. To do that, given the slim body of evidence then before me, I would have to educate myself in some new areas and also solve a string of connected mysteries. Some of those mysteries have been solved in the course of my research. The answers to others have rested on informed guesses, the logic of which I hope will become apparent in the text and notes. Still others, I'm afraid, including the authorship of the ballad, have remained mysteries, perhaps yet to be solved.

With the enthusiastic encouragement of James L. Garvin, New Hampshire's official state architectural historian, who at the outset saw more significance in the story than I did, and the eager help of Kate Reinhardt, my graduate assistant at the time and previously a fledgling architect, the necessary detective work began. Anyone who has ever experienced the gracious generosity, the resourcefulness, and the plain command of information in the mind and personality of Jim Garvin will not be surprised to learn that he cheerfully guided and served me as both mentor and research assistant, and has been indispensable in both roles as well as wonderfully pleasant company. Without Jim, this little book would not have been written. Kate Reinhardt is in part responsible for my decision to move this project to the front burner, as it were, and did most of the early archival research while keeping our notes and research materials organized. By her devotion to the project in its formative stages she has made it partly hers. Kate's successor as graduate assistant was Peter S. Leavenworth, whose background as a building contractor was a major asset in the effort to imagine and then reconstruct the practicalities of putting up the meetinghouse. Pete has contributed much, including his own store of materials on historic building techniques, more archival work, and several research reports on various aspects of the project. Though the formal responsibilities of two other graduate students, Bill Leavenworth and Karen Alexander, did not involve work on this project, I wish to acknowledge their interest, their valuable insights, their guided tour of Sheldrick Forest in Wilton, their assistance in related endeavors, and their sustaining friendship.

My acquaintance with the town of Wilton was greatly facilitated by Kate's accidental encounter at the New Hampshire Historical Society with John Hutchinson. John, with whom I had grown up in another New Hampshire community many years ago, had, in a happy coincidence, become something of an amateur historian during his long residence in Wilton, where he spent his career and now lives in retirement. He and his wife Marilyn not only showed me the lay of the land and provided valuable background but also put me in touch with others, most especially Helen Ring, whose work with the Wilton Historical Society and the First Church of Wilton yielded extremely useful materials, including a typescript of the church records and the only copy I have seen of what I believe to be the ballad's first appearance in print.

I have also greatly benefited from yet another fortuitous contact, this one with Clarke Blair of Fonda, New York. One of the tasks I assigned myself was to locate other copies of the ballad, hoping thereby to learn something about its transmission and mysterious authorship. I have been only partly successful in that quest, but bibliographical research led me to an article in *Yankee* magazine, published in 1970. The article was a brief treatment of the Wilton meetinghouse accident, based in part on a copy of the ballad owned by "the Clarke Blairs of central New York." The magazine did not have a record of the Blairs in its files, but its editor, Judson Hale, agreed to print a query from me. To my delight, Mr. Blair responded. When I met him at his home, Mr. Blair provided not only photographs of that copy, which had been in his New Hampshire–connected family for an unknown number of generations, but also an unexpected and useful discussion and subsequent correspondence on construction methods. He also led me to yet another valuable contact, Richard W. Babcock of Hancock, Massachusetts, a specialist in the restoration and reconstruction of old barns, whose correspondence has been both gracious and important. Mr. Blair's copy of the ballad has since been purchased by the University of New Hampshire library.

In support of my effort to explore the ballad and the questions surrounding it, several scholars have responded generously and helpfully to my queries: Sandy Ives of the University of Maine, Betty Bandel of the University of Vermont, Arthur Schrader of Southbridge, Massachusetts, and my colleague David Watters, who read and responded usefully to the entire manuscript. David made several important suggestions that I have followed.

I have already mentioned some people, beginning with Jim Garvin, who have been particularly helpful in my effort to understand the construction of a building that no longer exists. Others who have contributed to that effort have been Bruce Beckley, who showed several of us around the upper reaches of the Congregational Church building in Amherst, New Hampshire, the construction of which was supervised by the same Ephraim Barker who was master builder on the Wilton job; my brother Lew Clark of Beckett, Massachusetts; and Abbot Lowell Cummings, upon whose scholarship I have relied extensively and who graciously agreed to read the relevant parts of this manuscript. His comments were particularly helpful in enriching and clarifying my efforts to provide a glossary at the end of the book.

Obviously, none of those whose help and support I have acknowledged is responsible for any of my mistakes or omissions.

I reserve for special mention my cherished friend John Hatch, one of New England's most distinguished artists, whose interest in the project, meticulous care with details, and willingness to provide the most vital illustrations I had no right to expect but for which I am profoundly grateful. Some of the details of construction, and the final decision to accept a particular raising scenario as the most likely, emerged primarily from discussions with him.

The chief determinant of my professional life between 1993 and 1997 has been my appointment to the James H. Hayes and Claire Short Hayes Chair in the Humanities, established by Mr. Hayes not long before his death as the last in a long list of significant gifts to the University of New Hampshire. I had the honor to be the first incumbent, thereby acquiring greater flexibility of schedule and a succession of graduate assistants, both of which have been essential to the completion of this project.

As always, my wife Margery has been an interested and supportive companion on the little journeys, both literal and figurative, upon which the meetinghouse project has taken us. As always, she is indispensable.

Durham, New Hampshire   C.E.C.
Thanksgiving 1997

The Meetinghouse Tragedy

Prologue

❦ ❧

Attention give and you shall hear
A meloncholy theme
Tis such an instance as there is
But very seldom seen

In seventeen hundred seventy three
September seventh Day
At Wilton did Almity God
His anger there Display

Those ominous lines begin a handwritten ballad of forty-three stanzas, tucked by someone many generations ago into a family Bible. The folded sheets of the ballad are hand stitched to make a pamphlet, bearing at the end the name of the first owner: "Phebe Howard her verses given to her July ye 25, 1779." And as if to establish undoubted claim to this apparently proud possession, either she or the donor added, "Phebe Howard her Book and Name. All you that look may See the Same." Phebe, or Phoebe, was one of my great-great-great grandmothers, born in 1779, the very year that the pamphlet was "given to her." It has made its way to me by the transmission of the Bible across the generations on my mother's mother's mother's side. As it turns out, this is not the only surviving copy of the ballad, whose importance will eventually be made plain, but it is the one that introduced me to Wilton and the meetinghouse tragedy.

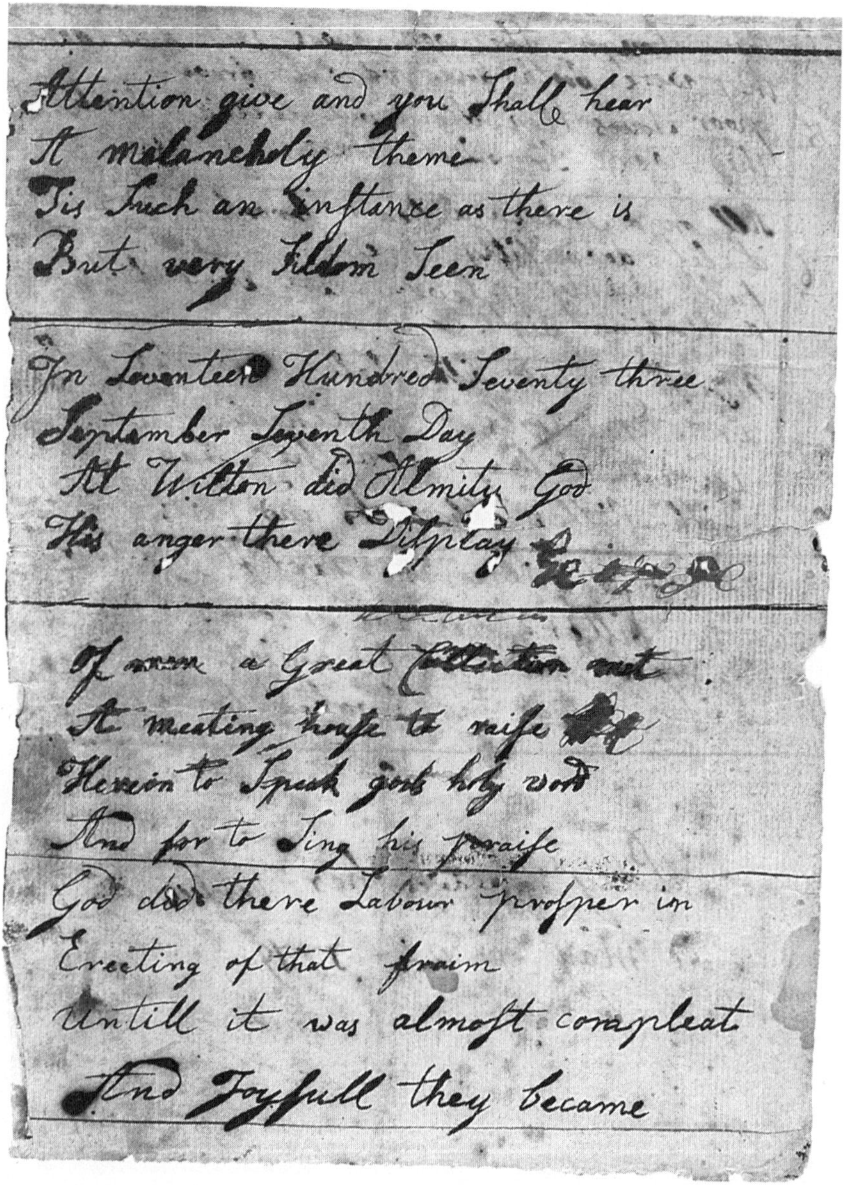

Attention give and you Shall hear
A melancholy theme
Tis Such an instance as there is
But very Seldom Seen

In Seventeen Hundred Seventy three
September Seventh Day
At Wilton did Almity God
His anger there Display

Of men a Great Collection met
At meeting house to raise
Herein to Speak gods holy word
And for to Sing his praise
God did there Labour prosper in
Erecting of that fraim
Untill it was almost compleat
And Joyfull they became

FIGURE 2(a) *The first page of the Polly Lewis–Phebe Howard copy of the ballad, owned by author. Photo by University of New Hampshire Photographic Services.*

they thought the worst was past and gone
they were booth bold and brave
poor Souls they did but little think
they were So nigh there graves

till on a Sudden a beam broak
it let down fifty three
full twenty Seven feet they fell
a Shocking Sight to See

Much timber with these men did fall
and Eged tools likewise
all in a heap together Lay
with bitter Shreeks and Cries

It would pierce the hardest heart to hear
the bitter Cries and grones
of them that in the ruins Lay
with wounds and brooken bones

Polly Lewis her Verses
may ye 24 — 1779

Polly Lewis her

(b)   *The second page of the ballad, showing ownership by Polly Lewis. Photo by University of New Hampshire Photographic Services.*

3

40 Let us be makeing peace with god
while we have life and breath
that Sowe may prepaired be
to meet a Sudden death

And be there by translated from
a world of misery
into a world of joy and bliss
to dwell with god on high

42 To drink of the clear Streams of Joy
that flow at gods right hand
and to injoy his heavenly Love
for ever without end

43 That this may be our happy case
When we this life do end
god grant of his Infinite grace
threw Jesus Christ Amen

Finis SSSSS Wilton September 1773

Phebe Howard her verses given to her July 29
1779

Phebe Howard her Book and Name
All you that Book may See the Same

(c) *The last page of the ballad, showing transfer of ownership to Phebe Howard. Photo by University of New Hampshire Photographic Services.*

4

Wilton

❧ ❧

Of men a Great Collection met
A meeting house to raise
Herein to speak god's holy word
And for to sing his praise.

The Great Collection of men consisted of 120 actual raisers from Wilton and elsewhere,[1] but that does not count the women, children, and older men of the town who gathered to give help and support, serve refreshments, and celebrate. A province census that year counted 580 members of this growing community, and no doubt a good share of them had come.[2] Colonel Reuben Kidder's "Old Caesar," one of the four slaves owned in nearby New Ipswich, was among those who watched in fascination while a mulatto man entertained the onlookers with magic tricks.[3] Almost certainly other performers, not to mention plain rowdy boys, added to the carnival atmosphere. The town had voted to provide six barrels of rum for the occasion, a detail that did not escape the attention of temperance-era town historians in the next century. The records, however, do not mention the enormous quantities of food that must also have been on hand, probably served by women and girls from booths or across long tables set up at the edge of the hilltop field where the frame lay ready for raising.[4] Like an annual militia muster, a town meeting, or an ordination, a meetinghouse raising was a community festival, made more memorable than the other three by its greater rarity and potential risk, and by the relative permanence of its very visible results. On previous occasions in Wilton, if a similar gathering had finished its job of raising the frame of a neighbor's house or barn before nightfall, young men and boys, their energies not yet exhausted, had kept the festivities going as long as possible with wrestling matches, quoits (played with iron rings), and a soccer-like game called "goal."[5] There would be no such games on this day.

Wilton, New Hampshire, lies west of the Merrimack Valley in the hilly ground that rises to meet the Monadnock region in the second tier of towns north of the boundary with Massachusetts that was drawn in 1741. A northern slice had once been a piece of one of the so-called Canada townships, granted by the Massachusetts Bay province in the 1730s to veterans, or their descendants, of a failed expedition to Quebec during the French wars. Its first settlers, along with neighbors who settled in the part of the grant that eventually became Lyndeborough, had come from Massachusetts, largely from Salem, in 1739. The rest of the town had been given in 1749 to another group of grantees, mostly from Andover, Massachusetts, by the so-called Masonian Proprietors, Portsmouth gentlemen who had just bought up, after more than a century of confusion, the great land claim of New Hampshire's first proprietor, Captain John Mason. That had been eight years after the boundary settlement resolved conflicting claims of jurisdiction in that area in favor of New Hampshire. Accordingly, when it came time for the residents to apply for incorporation and thus the legal and political privileges to which the status of "town" would entitle them, it had been New Hampshire's Governor Benning Wentworth who signed the act of incorporation and bestowed upon the new town the name of Wilton, perhaps after a sculptor Wentworth had known in London.[6] Wilton is bounded on the south by the border towns of Mason and Greenville, on the west by Temple, and on the east by Milford. In 1773 there was only Mason on the southern border, since Greenville was not yet separate from it, and the modern town of Milford was an unincorporated area known as Mile Slip. Lyndeborough, which contributed a heavy share of the raisers on that memorable September 7, lies just to the north.

By the time the two parts of Wilton were granted, and the rules for its settlement established, the government of Massachusetts had abandoned an earlier effort, never adopted by New Hampshire, to enforce compact settlement by requiring proprietors to lay out small "home lots" in a village, where all settlers were expected to live, and then add to each "right" one or more large

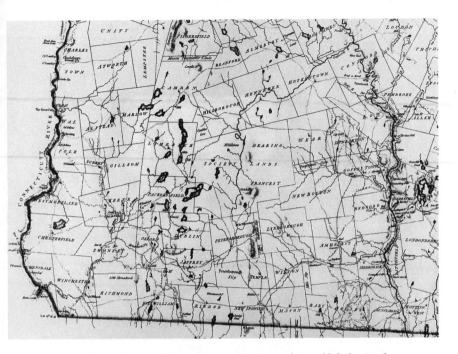

FIGURE 3. *Part of the so-called Holland map of New Hampshire, published in London in 1784 from data collected several years earlier. This piece shows part of the southwest quadrant of the province. Wilton is near the bottom of the map, just north of Mason. The location of the meetinghouse is indicated by a stylized representation of a church. The map is entitled "A Topographical Map of the Province of New Hampshire. Surveyed for Samuel Holland, Esq., His Majesty's Surveyor General of Lands for the Northern District of North America." Photo by University of New Hampshire Photographic Services from a copy in Special Collections, UNH Library.*

farming or wood lots in a series of "after divisions." The result would have been an adaptation of the "open field" system, one method of allotting farmland in manorial England.[7] The method had never really worked in northern New England, even when this part of New Hampshire and all of Maine were still part of Massachusetts, because most settlers had come in search of land and elbow room and wanted to develop their farms immediately and live on them from the beginning. Therefore, settlers violated the rules.[8] Nor would such a system suit the speculative purposes of the Masonian proprietors.

Accordingly, Wilton, like all the other townships granted after 1741 either by the Masonian Proprietors or by Governor Went-

worth, had been laid out checkerboard style, this one in two hundred eighty-acre lots arranged in ten ranges. Three lots had been
claimed by each of the original grantees, and by each of the Masonian proprietors themselves, by drawing.[9] Each settler, whether
an original grantee or a subsequent purchaser, had cleared his
land and built his house on a part of one of his lots wherever it
happened to be, regardless of its proximity to others. And there
was still plenty of space to fill. If about sixty acres was the optimum farming and woodlot space for a single family—an estimate
offered by Darrett B. Rutman for this time and place—Wilton
could double its number of households before it had arrived at the
full effective use of available land, even if it continued to be ex-
clusively a farming community.[10] Whenever a grouping of buildings had come to appear over the years—and that process was
just barely underway at the time of the meetinghouse raising—it
had been in response to commercial or social needs conditioned
by geography and historical accident rather than by adherence to
a prearranged scheme. While not prescribing a village, however,
the Masonian grantors had directed its grantees to provide for a
civic center, and told them indirectly where it should be.

Like most towns in New England, Wilton now contains within
its twenty-five square miles several distinct clusters of inhabitants
as well as a scattered rural population. Wilton Center, the site of
the raising, ceased to be the principal village of the town when the
railroad and water power from the Souhegan River combined in
the nineteenth century to create a busy mill village in the valley
two miles northeast of the hilltop. In 1773, however, Wilton Center, on a hill twelve miles north of the Massachusetts line, was the
center of the town in fact as well as in name, and was intended to
be from the beginning. The Masonian Proprietors had designated
Lot 11 in Range 5, right in the geographic center of the town, as
the "meeting house lot," and ordained as one condition of the
grant that a six-acre square in the southwest corner of the lot be
set aside for "public purposes."[11] It could hardly have been accidental that the six-acre square thus designated was so topographi-
cally well suited to its function. From this high clearing, some
seven hundred feet above sea level, the raising party could view
some of Wilton's higher land to the east across the Souhegan Val-

ley. By looking a little over five miles to the northwest, just north of Temple Mountain, they could see Pack Monadnock, at two thousand one hundred feet the most conspicuous local landmark.

A dirt road, cart-rutted and seasoned with ox and horse dung, ran over the hilltop on the eastern edge of the clearing. It connected with another road three-quarters of a mile to the north to form a junction where John Cram, Jr., lived with his wife, Susannah, and their three young children. The house had been built by John's father, one of the three men elected in 1762 to serve as the town's first selectmen. An informal network of such roads, each laid out by vote of the town as the occasion arose, cut through the first-growth forests of giant pines and hardwoods and across cleared meadows and fields to connect the scattered farms and small clusters of houses.

The network was slightly more complex north of the meeting-house lot than south of it, since that part of town had been settled longer. Here on some of the northernmost lots, in what was once part of Lyndeborough, lived some of the emigrants who had come beginning in 1739 to "Salem Canada," as that proprietary township was known before its incorporation in 1764. Among these early settlers were John Bales, John Dale, John Badger, Alexander Milliken, and the Putnam brothers, Jacob and Ephraim, each with their families. Either they or their sons still occupied homesteads in this part of town in 1773. In the next generation, these pioneer settlers and their early neighbors, such as the Burton brothers, John Jr. and Jonathan, and Ephraim Butterfield, all of whom would frequently hold town offices, would be outnumbered by the newly arrived Andover group, consisting largely of newly married couples in their twenties. In fact, reported an Andover town history of 1829, no fewer than sixty Andover men "who were, or became heads of families" had settled in Wilton.[12] According to the logic of random lot-drawing, the farms of these more recent settlers were not confined to any one section of the town, but most of the newcomers established their farmsteads in the eastern rather than the western ranges. Some of these were fairly close to the meetinghouse, but many others were on the high ground across the Souhegan, with some clustering in the southeast corner of the town near Mile Slip, well removed from

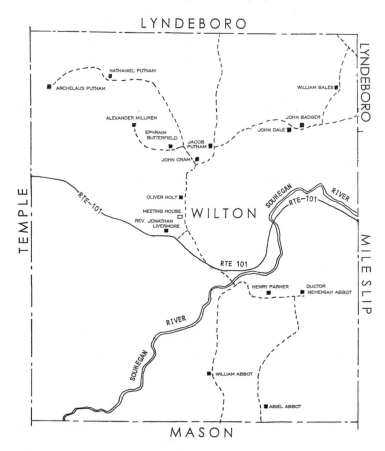

FIGURE 4.   *Map of Wilton, c. 1773. The locations of only a few of the roughly 120 house-holds are shown. Modern New Hampshire Route 101, represented by a solid line, is shown for the purpose of orientation. The modern village of Wilton is located along the Souhegan River toward the eastern edge of the town. The meetinghouse was at Wilton Center, shown near the center of the map. Drawing by John W. Hatch.*

the northern lots of the earlier settlers and some three to four miles from the meetinghouse.

Among the Andover group living in the vicinity of the meeting-house common were several members of the Holt family, including thirty-three-year-old Oliver Holt with his wife Eunice and their children Eunice and Oliver, nine and seven. The most prominent of the Andover settlers in the southeast neighborhood was Abiel Abbot, at thirty-two already elected selectman five times and headed for a long career in public service. James Brown, another frequent selectman, lived in this corner of town as well. Also on the east side of the river but farther north than the Abbot and Brown farms lived George Lancey with his wife, Elizabeth, three months away from delivering their third child—not counting little William, who had died in infancy five years before.[13]

Near where the new meetinghouse frame was laid out in that clearing atop Wilton Center stood the town's twenty-one-year-old log meetinghouse, now too small to fulfill either of its two intended functions: the conduct of civic affairs and the public worship of God. That is why the town had voted just a year earlier to build a new one in its place.[14] Eventually, the town would sell the old building at auction, the materials to be carted away.[15] For now it was here that the townspeople of Wilton, or rather those of its 121 adult males who turned out to do so, transacted public business at frequent town meetings, summoned by the town constable's official publication of the meeting warrant that was drawn up on each occasion by the three selectmen.[16]

At each regular annual meeting in March, the voters elected the selectmen and the numerous other officers and committees necessary to serve a New England town during the year. In March 1773 they had elected three new selectmen, William Abbot, Jr., Abner Stiles, and Jonathan Martin. Abbot and Stiles were among Wilton's most frequent officeholders. This was Martin's first term as a selectman, but in the year to come he would have the honor of being elected one of Wilton's two representatives to New Hampshire's new Provincial Congress.

Despite the democratic ethos that is implied by the system of annual elections, the 121 male voters of Wilton did not distribute the leadership of the town very broadly among themselves. We lack tax records for the first decades of the town's existence, so we cannot tell to what extent election to the offices of selectman, moderator, town clerk, and treasurer depended upon economic status. But between 1762 and 1775, a total of only twenty-three men served in one of these top offices. Of those, thirteen served more than once. John Burton, Jr., and Abiel Abbot each served as selectman five times; Burton was also town clerk for eleven years and Abbot was elected once to the Provincial Congress. Abbot, the most prominent of the Andover settlers, was a perennial militia officer and over the years to come would serve a total of sixteen years as a deacon of the Wilton church. Five others served as selectman three times or more. Thus the actual leadership of this self-governing community, as in most New England towns, rested in the hands of quite a narrow segment of the community.[17]

One annual meeting was not enough to handle the rather complex affairs of a self-governing community whose only officials were part-time amateurs, each with carefully delineated responsibilities. The selectmen summoned a special town meeting whenever the need arose; in 1773 there were six. On April 20, for example, the meeting voted to lay out six roads, the route of each described more or less as follows: "Beginning at the Southerly side of [the] Road leading from Timothy Dales to Jacob Putnams Mill at or near the corner of Nehemiah Abbots Pasture Fence so on Southerly in the most convenient Place to the Mill Brook so called. Said Road is to be Two Rods [thirty-three feet] Wide."[18] At this and other meetings, in addition to taking various actions on the major town project of the year, the new meetinghouse, the voters among other business reviewed the accounts of the town treasurer, appropriated money for holding a school that year, decided to repair some bridges and to build a pound, and approved a somewhat complicated transaction between the town and John Cram involving land for a new "burying place."[19] Each expenditure of money had to be met by imposing a "rate" on each of the 121 voters (called "polls") and the assessed worth of each man's property, to be collected by the constable.

Twice each Sunday, and on fast and thanksgiving days proclaimed by town or province whenever the occasion seemed to demand it, the community gathered at the meetinghouse for divine worship. The weekly gathering, for it was really one meeting broken into morning and afternoon sessions by an interlude for socializing and eating a cold lunch, was far more than a religious observance alone. It was an important element, perhaps the one indispensable element, in the community's ritual affirmation of itself—consisting above all in a gathering of neighbors.

A nineteenth-century historian of Wilton got it right when he observed that "society has grown less neighborly, but more philanthropic." He meant that village life, organized charities, reform movements, mission societies, fraternal societies, fairs and exhibitions, Sunday School picnics, church suppers, day excursions by rail, and even vacation trips had by his day replaced older, perhaps more natural forms of socializing and of doing good.[20] The life of Wilton in the 1770s, like that of most country towns in the region, was a life shared by neighbors, however widely separated their farmsteads lay. Coming together by means of primitive rural roads was difficult and time-consuming, and demanded planning, both in working out the logistics of the family's movements and in accommodating farm chores and projects to the occasion. Such obstacles rendered communal occasions all the more significant to the life of the town and to its members, both psychologically and as matters of practical necessity, as when neighbors gathered to husk corn, work up an annual woodpile, or put up the frame of a house or a barn on one another's behalf. To attempt any of these chores single-handedly would be either a prohibitively poor use of time or, in the last case, physically impossible. Thus the town was not only a family-centered society founded upon private property and individual enterprise, but a communal society as well. The distinctive ethos that resulted was perhaps never better captured than in the homely term "neighborliness."

There was a distinctive female side to this communalism in addition to the women's supporting role in the largely male activities just mentioned. The classic instance, of course, is the matter of childbirth, an occasion that gathered not just the immediate family and a professional midwife, but also a substantial gathering of experienced and concerned neighboring wives. By raising day, there had been at least seventeen occasions in 1773 for this neighborly and distinctly feminine ritual.[21] There would be three more before the end of December, one of them tragically in the shadow of the events of September 7. In towns such as this, neighboring women frequently borrowed kitchen staples and appliances from one another and came together regularly to share in homely tasks such as spinning, shelling peas, berrying, and washing clothes, as well as in the better known and more formally organized activities such as quilting bees.[22]

Abiel Abbot, eldest son of one of the Andover group that had

settled Wilton in the 1760s, was three months short of his eighth
birthday on the raising day in 1773. On the occasion of the town's
centennial in 1839, he published some of his childhood recollections, including visits by neighbors, who "were always asked to
drink beer and cider." He also recalled afternoon gatherings of
women eager to share one another's company even while engaged
in individual domestic chores: "When women visited their neighbors, they went early in the afternoon, carried their work, and returned home before sundown to take care of milking the cows,
and so forth. Their entertainment was commonly shortcake baked
by the fire, and tea, except in the early part of the Revolutionary
war. For the visit they often put on a clean chequered apron and
handkerchief and short loose gown." While it may be that the
writer's boyhood memories wore the romantic haze of time, his
summary of the quality of neighborliness in the decade before the
Revolution offers at least some confirmation of the communal nature of town society.

Our fathers and mothers were benevolent, hospitable and kind; the stranger
was received . . . with a hearty welcome. In their own neighborhood and
town, they were all brothers and sisters. There was an admirable equality, a
home-feeling and a heart-feeling among all. Their visits were not formal, cer-
emonious and heartless, but frank, cheerful and cordial. Their sympathy for
the sick, unfortunate and distressed was expressed by their ready assistance
and kindly affectioned help. When prosperous all partook in the common
joy; when sickness or calamity befell any, all were affected, the sorrow was
mutual, and aid and relief, as far as possible, were afforded. They were indeed one family—all members of one sympathizing body.[23]

The most frequent, and most overtly ceremonial, of neighborly
gatherings was the weekly one at the meetinghouse. It was also
the most inclusive, since participation was not limited by either
age or gender. The only distinction within this town congregation
was between those who were and those who were not members of
the church. Everyone's attendance was expected, and absences
noted and sometimes discussed. Piety, of course, was not universal, but attendance at meeting was nearly so. No doubt the as-
semblage included a good many "horse shed Christians," to use
David Hall's term,[24] and chances are that many of the adults and
most of the children found the noon-time interval the high point

of the day. But the preaching of the Reverend Jonathan Livermore
was not theologically demanding, though it was occasionally con-
troversial, and a surprisingly large proportion of the townspeople
took their religious commitment seriously enough to be members
of the church.

The church was a covenanted body of professed Christian be-
lievers, both men and women, which had been gathered according to New England custom in 1763, the same year the town was
incorporated. Its records between then and the end of the first
pastor's ministry in 1777 have been lost, making it hard to know
how many of Wilton's 580 people were members of the church in
1773. Twenty-seven men had signed the first covenant ten years
earlier, but a published church report of 1824 points out that the
signers did not include all of the first members.

For one thing, in keeping with the practice of the time, the signatures include the names of no female members, who may actually have outnumbered their brethren.[25] Bathsheba Blanchard, after all, had been one of the two people—her husband Nathan
was the other—to whom we can trace a first crucial step in the
forming of the church, with legitimacy, according to New England practice. Nathan and Bathsheba, who had moved to Wilton
along with many of their former neighbors from Andover, had
both been "dismissed" from their home church in Andover in 1763
specifically in order to "form a church in Wilton."[26] Nor, says the
1824 report, did the signers even include many of the men. In all,
according to this later claim, the signers comprised only about
"one fourth of the members."[27]

If this is so, the church had about one hundred members upon
its organization. The town had grown by between eighty and
ninety percent since then. Despite the fact that much of Wilton's
new population consisted of children born over the past ten years
who would not join the church until adolescence, Mr. Livermore
added 152 persons to the membership during his thirteen-year
pastorate, which ended in 1777. Allowing for an unknown number
of deaths and "removals" among the original membership, and
noting that in 1773 almost thirty percent of Mr. Livermore's pastorate was yet to come, we can still guess that by the time of the

raising, the church had around two hundred members—an unusually large proportion (one-third) of all the men, women, and children in the town.[28]

Membership in the church demanded none of the tests of visible sainthood of the previous century. One needed only to be free from scandal, subscribe to a covenant drawn up in 1763 that expressed belief in a Trinitarian and Biblical, but not specifically Calvinist, deity, and promise to submit to the discipline of the church. To apply technical terms, the statement of faith in the covenant could be described as both Arminian and Latitudinarian. Both the gathering of the church and the ordination of its first minister took place after the fires of the Great Awakening and its controversies had subsided, but like most southern New Hampshire churches and ministers who had actually come through that tempestuous era in organized form, this community and its spiritual leader were clearly "Old Light" in temper.[29] This relatively loose theological atmosphere cannot but have been congenial to most of the young Andover group, many of whom had come of age under the tutelage of the Reverend William Symmes, the long-term respected minister of Andover, whose opinions were described in an early history of that town as "accord[ing] rather with Arminius, than with Calvin; and with Arius rather than Athanasius."[30]

The leader of the Wilton congregation was the Reverend Mr. Livermore, whose rather grand clapboarded Georgian house stood just down the hill to the south of the meetinghouse site.[31] Mr. Livermore, forty-one, had graduated in 1760 from Harvard, which he had entered at the almost unheard-of advanced age of twenty-six, ranking socially near the bottom of his class upon admission.[32] As did most New England ministers, he served both as pastor of his gathered flock and as an officer of the town—its official "teacher of morality and piety," to use the words of the New Hampshire Constitution that would be adopted in the next decade. Thus he had been called—and was subject to dismissal—by both church and town in separate actions. Wilton, however, may have been unusual in the extent to which church and town overlapped, since a comparatively large proportion of the townspeople seem also to have been members of the church.[33] It was the town that determined his salary and raised the taxes to pay it. After ten years in office in Wilton, Mr. Livermore was the object of some discontent, on grounds that are unclear. In the April before the meetinghouse raising, a town meeting, responding to what seems almost a gratuitous warrant article citing his "promise" that he would seek acceptance of his resignation should he become aware that "the Major Part of the People of . . . [the] Town were Dissatisfied with him," voted "to give the Revnd. Mr. Livermore a Dismission Provided he should ask one."[34] He did not "ask one" in 1773, nor did his troubles with the community, whatever they may have been at this point, come to a head for another five years.

Church membership entailed certain privileges not available to the town at large, the most important of which was access to the sacraments of Baptism and the Lord's Supper. Five times a year, following one of the public services of preaching, singing, and praying, the fellowship of the church separated itself from the larger community to experience more intimately the presence of Christ in the solemn Communion of bread and wine. At one of the Sunday services, Mr. Livermore and his successors often baptized one or more infant children of church members, sprinkling them with water from a basin in a symbolic cleansing that constituted their entry into what was presumed would be a Christian life, though actual membership in the church would come, if it did, much later. In 1779, the year after Mr. Livermore ended his ministry, his successor baptized forty-five children ranging in age from two days to one month—average age 8.6 days—in addition to the two children of Abraham and Ruth Butterfield, who had been admitted to the church two months earlier, and three of the four children of Benjamin and Annah Parker on the same day that Annah was admitted to membership. Two adults were also baptized on the occasion of their admittance to the church.[35]

Membership also entailed the privilege and duty of exercising—and submitting to—the discipline of the church. The fifteen missing years of church records would most likely disclose the same general pattern of church actions that are apparent in the years after 1778. The substance of most church meetings had

nothing to do with finances, except for the small amounts collected from members annually to pay for the Communion elements. Worldly finances, even when they affected the life of the
church, were the town's business. The church dealt with the acceptance of new members, the dismission of those who were
moving or wished to join other churches (a request not always
granted), and the punishment of offenses ranging from absence
from Communion to grave public scandal such as habitual drunk-
enness or "breaches of the 7th Commandment." During Mr. Livermore's day, candidates for admission who had committed this
last sin were required to make a public confession of their guilt
before they were admitted, a rule that was abandoned in 1804.[36]
Punishments for the various violations of discipline ranged from
"admonition" to censure and temporary suspension from church
privileges to, rarely, excommunication. The church also, usually
through a committee appointed for the purpose, strove to recon-
cile disputes between members, for members of the covenanted
community were expected to live in harmony and in Christian
charity with one another. Thus the church, in its more rigorous
and specifically theological way, reflected the neighborly values of
the larger community of which it was a part.

This community of neighbors, whose common life was largely
centered on its own and adjacent towns, to which the spirit of
neighborliness extended, was nevertheless connected in various
ways to the world outside Wilton, Lyndeborough, Temple, and
Mason . Some had relatives in other places, especially in Andover,
Massachusetts, whence many Wilton people had come. Most
farmers traded "down below," as they called Boston and the seaports of the Massachusetts North Shore, exchanging farm prod-
ucts for provisions that could not be raised at home.[37] Wilton had
no established postal route through the town until 1788,[38] and we
know little of the circulation of mail and newspapers in 1773. This
was still a very young community, which had yet to develop any
of the various institutions of information-sharing such as those
discussed by William J. Gilmore in his study of the upper Connecticut Valley region in the decades immediately ahead.[39] It is,
however, inconceivable that those who had friends and relatives
in northeastern Massachusetts did not find ways to communicate

with them, or that farmers on trading journeys to Boston did not bring back newspapers and oral reports of current affairs.

Certainly the townspeople of Wilton were well aware in 1773 that they lived in troubled times. Boston, their principal market town, had been an occupied city for five years. It had been three and a half years since some of the occupying soldiers had shot and killed five members of a rioting mob in what was even then being called the Boston "massacre." Even in their own provincial capital of Portsmouth, the once-popular John Wentworth, Benning's handsome nephew and successor as royal governor in 1767, was facing opposition and resistance born of resentment of the abuses of British authority elsewhere, to which the young governor seemed unable or unwilling to respond. Committees of Correspondence were being formed in some of New Hampshire's coastal communities, and now the news of the Tea Act, passed by Parliament in May, had filtered through the colonies and the townspeople of Wilton were joining in the universal boycott.[40]

As yet there had been no formal occasion to test individual loyalty to Crown or resistance effort. There is no question, however, that this community of neighbors, centered as it was on the concerns of town rather than empire and acutely conscious of what were widely seen as hostile acts by an alien authority in its trading center of Boston, was sympathetic as a whole to the American cause. Resistance to the King, in fact, may have seemed less unnatural to this young generation of former Andover men who had declared their economic independence from their fathers and removed themselves from parental authority by moving to Wilton than to an older and less mobile population.[41] Ten months in the future, on July 15, 1774, the town meeting would vote to participate in New Hampshire's choice of delegates to the First Continental Congress, to adopt an elaborate "covenant" signifying the town's participation in non-importation and non-consumption agreements, and to raise seventeen pounds "to provide the town's stock of ammunition."[42] More definitive proof would come two and a half years later when New Hampshire's Committee of Safety, executive of the temporary Revolutionary government, circulated a document throughout the province asking all adult males to sign a statement pledging to oppose hostile acts of Brit-

ish forces "at the Risque of our Lives and Fortunes, with Arms."
Of Wilton's 132 white men over the age of twenty-one, only two
dared defy the community consensus by refusing to sign.[43]

In September 1773, however, as far as towns like Wilton were
concerned, the situation had not yet reached the boiling point. For
now, the town's main expression of readiness for resistance was in
the local militia company, part of New Hampshire's 22nd Regi-
ment, of which Philip Putnam, a Wilton man, was colonel. The
Wilton company, commanded by Captain Jonathan Burton, was
composed, according to province law, of all the town's able-bodied
men,[44] who held periodic drills and the annual muster on the
same town common on which the meetinghouse was now being
raised. Thus the town militia company joined the town meeting,
the town church, and all the less formal acts of association and
neighborliness as another expression, another ritual affirmation,
of the communal side of Wilton's identity.

Early in the morning of Tuesday, September 7, in the open
plain atop Wilton Center, the geographic focus of Wilton's communal identity, a carpenter named Ephraim Barker assembled his
crew. The stage was now set for the meetinghouse tragedy.

The Meetinghouse

♨ ♩

God did there Labour prosper in
Erecting of that fraim
Untill it was almost compleat
And joyfull they became

*E*phraim Barker was in command. He was the master builder, a professional carpenter hired by the town to build the new meetinghouse.[1] For Barker, this was not an unfamiliar task. He had put up meetinghouses and barns in other New Hampshire communities before, including the Stratham and Pembroke meetinghouses and the one nearing completion in Amherst. Now in Wilton, following only the most general specifications voted by the town meeting and under the supervision of a seven-man building committee, Barker had the responsibility of getting the job done. To-day's raising, with 120 strong confident men to coordinate in a difficult and dangerous operation, marked the climax, though not the end, of a sequence of demanding tasks for the master builder. Before the raising had come the framing, and before the framing the cutting and the assembling of the timbers, and before that the designing of the building in accordance with the town's desires, and the planning of the complicated logistics leading up to the raising day.

The historian looking into the Wilton meetinghouse tragedy is handicapped by the absence of certain evidence. For one thing, the building no longer stands, having burned to the ground in 1859.[2] Fire has thus deprived us of what otherwise would be the key to its design and the details of its construction, including the species of its building materials. For another, even documentary records are sparse, especially compared to the riches available in some other communities. In the New Hampshire town of Wash-

ington, for example, two sensitive historians, aided by physical remains in good condition, recently wrote a marvelously circum-
stantial account of the building of the town meetinghouse of 1789,
largely on the basis of the detailed book of records kept by the
building committee.[3] No such document remains for Wilton. Nor
are the remaining official town records, consisting as they do of
concise town meeting reports and little else, as rich in the particu-
lars of building the meetinghouse as those, for example, of the adjoining town of New Ipswich or of nearby Marlborough.[4] Despite
these handicaps, much can be told—though on occasion the historian must resort to an informed guess.

On September 1, 1772, almost exactly a year before the raising
day, the voters of Wilton ordered up their new meetinghouse,
specifying only its location and its dimensions.[5] It was to stand
five rods, or a little over eighty feet, north of the existing log building. It was to be rather large, somewhat on the high side of the
range of meetinghouse dimensions of this generation in the region—sixty feet long, forty-five feet wide, and twenty-seven feet
from foundation to eaves. The five-year-old New Ipswich meetinghouse, with identical dimensions except that the post was
twenty-six instead of twenty-seven feet, was then "the largest
building within twenty miles."[6] One cannot help wondering
whether there was an element of civic pride involved in the decision to make the largest building in Wilton, its principal expression of civic identity, just a foot higher than that of its near neighbor. Today, discernible in 1997 on close examination of the site,
lie the remains of the rock-filled trench upon which the building's
foundation once rested. These remains, now covered by a gravel
parking lot, make it clear that the builder adhered faithfully to the
town's instructions for the ground plan, while several contemporary accounts confirm the use of twenty-seven-foot posts. The
pitch of the roof, disclosed in a nineteenth-century model of the
building and confirmed by its standard use in other meetinghouses of the time and region, was what modern builders call
"eight-over-twelve" (or more simply, just "eight"), which means
that for every foot of width between side plate and centered king
post, the roof rose eight inches. Thus the ridgepole ended up

fifteen feet above the plate. In all, therefore, the Wilton meeting-house was forty-two feet high.

In many other New England towns of the era, disputes among neighborhood factions over locating the meetinghouse sometimes raged for years and ended only with appeals to the province gov-ernment and the formation of separate parishes, but the choice of Wilton's new meetinghouse site apparently presented no prob-lem. The voters simply took it for granted that the hilltop center of the town, already referred to specifically in the vote of 1772 as the "Common," would be the location. That is where the original meetinghouse had stood for twenty years and where the town built the stone animal pound, still standing there today, that the voters would authorize on April 20, 1773.[7]

The building would be much like those in most of Wilton's neighboring towns, all of which were now being built according to essentially the same plan. Vernacular meetinghouse design in southern New England had begun to shift shortly before 1720 from the four-square hipped roof pattern of the late seventeenth century to a rectangular plan with gabled roof. In the northern New England interior, where most settlement came after 1720, the newer standard design was either the first to appear in a com-munity or, as in the case of Wilton and most of southern New Hampshire between the Merrimack and the Connecticut, a per-manent replacement for a small temporary structure, usually of one story and sometimes built of hewn logs. The main door was invariably centered in one of the long sides, apparently always the south side, and the pulpit in the opposite north side. Standard de-sign provided for an interior gallery stretching across the long side opposite the pulpit and along both of the narrow ends of the building. There were always windows at both the main and gallery levels, and a special window centered on the north wall at an in-termediate level to form a backdrop (and light) for the raised pul-pit. In some cases, perhaps the majority, the galleries were reached by enclosed stairs in two-story "porches" attached either to one or both ends of the building or to the front entrance. In re-cent years, one of the end porches in some cases had evolved into a tower extending to the peak of the roof or beyond, surmounted

FIGURE 5.   *Site of the meetinghouse at Wilton Center. The 1773 meetinghouse was located in the open space between the present First Church, on the right, which was its replacement, and the other white building to the left. Until 1997, when the space was covered with gravel for a parking lot, the remains of the foundation were discernible. The view is from the northeast. Photo by author.*

by an open belfry or a slim steeple—the first step, architecturally speaking, in the decades-long regional transition from meetinghouse to church.[8] In Wilton, the selectmen tried twice for approval of a two-porch design and once even suggested a steeple, but had managed so far to pry authorization for only one porch out of the reluctant voters. It was to be on the "foreside," which archeological evidence and a photograph of a long-missing nineteenth-century model of the building both suggest must have meant not at the main entrance on the south side but on the east end facing the road.[9] Whether the stairs in this single porch provided the only access to the gallery or whether there may have been another set of stairs inside the main structure at the opposite end, we shall probably never know.

Rural meetinghouses of the period could be painted or unpainted, but if painted were usually yellow, orange, blue, or green, most commonly some shade of yellow, often with a dull red roof, called "Spanish brown." The meetinghouse need not have been of one color alone. Not only were the roof shingles, doors, windows,

FIGURE 6. *Photograph of a model of the Wilton meetinghouse, showing Victorian embellishments to what was once probably the east "porch," subsequently converted to a tower. These changes were probably made about 1832, the year the building acquired a bell. The model is no longer extant. The photograph is from Abiel Abbot Livermore and Sewall Putnam,* History of the Town of Wilton (*Lowell, Mass.: Marden & Rowell, 1888*).

FIGURE 7. *The meetinghouse in Sandown, New Hampshire, erected in 1773, the year of the Wilton meetinghouse raising. Photo by author.*

FIGURE 8. *The meetinghouse in Fremont, New Hampshire (1800), showing two end "porches" or enclosed stairways of the type that were apparently attached to the eastern and western ends of the Wilton meetinghouse at some time in its history, though not necessarily at the time of the raising. Photo by author.*

and trim usually treated differently from the clapboard siding, but some communities even gave different colors to one side of the building than to others. Although it has now become a commonplace among the cognoscenti that the ubiquitous white paint of the Greek and colonial revivals was not a feature of the eighteenth century, an occasional white meetinghouse could be seen even then.[10] As for the Wilton meetinghouse, we know only that sometime between 1774 and 1781 it was painted *something*, apparently more than one color. At the end of 1781, the voters of Temple voted to "colour" their new meetinghouse "in its several parts, agreeable to Wilton meeting-house colours . . ."[11]

A month after the momentous decision to commit the town to a new meetinghouse, the voters began to get down to details. There would be a special tax levy to raise 150 pounds for building materials, specifically including timber, boards, shingles, and stones. Every "rated" person in the town, meaning everyone who paid taxes, was to have the chance to bid on providing these various materials, the contracts to go at "vendue" to the lowest bidders. At the same time, the voters elected a committee to take charge of this provision of materials and to "build the house": John

Burton, Jr., Jonathan Martin, Joseph Butterfield, John Stevens, Abiel Abbot, Samuel Pettengill, and Abner Stiles.[12] If the meetinghouse plan was essentially standard in this part of New England toward the end of the eighteenth century, the same cannot be said about procurement methods for materials. Wilton, as we have just seen, directed the building committee to buy them with public money from the lowest resident bidders, who would do the cutting and the hauling and hire whatever crews would be necessary to meet their contracts. In other cases it was the building committee that organized the work of supplying timbers and boards without such detailed instructions from the town, and in still others it was the master builder. In some towns the residents themselves, instead of being assessed a special tax as the Wilton taxpayers were, cut and assembled the framing and building materials directly.[13]

There was one more important preparation the town had to make. On June 3, at the same meeting that authorized the building of one porch, the voters took action on "providing Entertainment for the Raisers," as the selectmen phrased it in the warrant. The building committee was put in charge of that detail after the meeting voted to provide:

one Barrel of West India Rum
Five Barrels of New England Rum
One Barrel of Good Brown Sugar
Half a Box of Good Lemons
Two Loves of Loaf Sugar, for Framing and Raseing sd. Meeting House.[14]

Assuming the better quality West India rum was intended to be drunk neat by those who scorned the alternative, the five barrels of cheaper rum with water and sugar and lemons in the quantities voted could have made several hundred gallons of rum punch. At a raising in Rockingham, Vermont, in 1787, such a mixture filled a washtub, from which the raisers helped themselves with tin dippers.[15]

To frame a meetinghouse of the stated dimensions, Barker needed up to two hundred large pine and oak trees, together weighing fifty or more tons depending on the combination of wood.[16] In northern New England, the favored framing material was the white pine with which the region abounds. There were especially rich stands of first-growth pine in Wilton, some of which have actually persevered through the masting industry of the eighteenth century and the sheep craze of the nineteenth to our day.[17] The second most common framing material was oak, used more extensively than pine in southern New England because it was more available there. Oak is twice as heavy as pine, and therefore much more difficult to handle. Moreover, although there was (and is) plenty of oak to be found in the predominantly softwood forests of the north, it was harder to find sufficiently straight lengths of oak for the longest timbers than of pine. On the other hand, as was readily recognized at the time, oak is stronger. The builders of northern New England, therefore, even when building mainly of pine, often used oak for the most crucial members of the frame, especially when erecting a large building such as a barn or a meetinghouse.[18] Even without the slightest bit of material or documentary evidence for confirmation, we can therefore speculate with reasonable safety that Barker and the building committee chose white pine, perhaps augmented by some spruce and hemlock, for the greater part of the frame, but oak timbers for at least the twelve twenty-seven-foot vertical posts that would carry the combined weight of massive plates and tie beams in addition to the rafter assemblies and other elements of the roof structure.[19]

By late October 1772, the "vendue" presumably having taken place perhaps two or three weeks after the authorizing vote of October 5 (the committee was required to give a week's notice for the occasion), the successful bidders would have been ready to begin felling the giant pines and oaks from which the framing timbers would be hewn. This schedule of events was not far from the one followed fourteen years later in Washington, where cutters were directed not only to fell their trees in September and October, but to do so "in the old of the moon." Both directives sprang from ancient folk wisdom, the first of which the historians of the Washington meetinghouse suggest was related to the effects of cold weather on the curing process and the second of which they think may not have been taken seriously.[20] A more practical reason for getting the logs ready for hauling before winter was that snow on the ground would make it far easier to skid them by ox team out of the woods.

Once the great trees were felled and hauled to the framing site, they had to be shaped into the squared timbers that would make up the meetinghouse frame. In some building projects of the day, workmen hewed logs into timbers without bothering to remove the bark first. One can still find floor joists, especially, which were often hewn flat on the top side only, still bearing bark on the un-hewn parts. If most of the Wilton logs were stripped before hew-ing, as they may have been, the job was done with a long-handled device known as a bark spud, supplemented by a shorter peeling chisel and adze. Had the cutting waited until spring when the sap was running, pine and spruce bark would have slipped away from the glistening wood with little effort by the workman, making the job almost a pleasure. However, the advantages of fall cutting, namely a longer time for drying and the coming snow and ice cover for transportation, almost certainly outweighed the fact that the dryer bark of autumn was a bit more stubborn. Even more to the point, the process had to begin in time to assemble the hun-dreds of processed logs that would be needed to begin the fram-ing process in the spring or early summer. In the case of the oak, it is easy to imagine that the bark was removed more carefully in order to make it usable for grinding into the essential ingredient for some local farmer's tanning pit. This would have been done by ringing the bark into three-foot lengths with a special tool called a barking axe before removing the pieces with the spud.[21] With the bark removed, or possibly even without that operation, the logs that would form the larger members of the frame—sills, posts, plates, tie beams, principal rafters, and king posts—were hewn by hand, primarily with the carpenter's broad axe, a much heavier tool than the axe used for felling. The smaller timbers such as studs, purlins, braces of various kinds, and secondary rafters were probably cut out by vertical saw at one of Wilton's wa-ter-powered sawmills.[22]

All this was hard, time-consuming work, some of it demanding specialized skills. No doubt Barker's hired crew of carpenters did most of it. Logs still containing most of their sap, weighing up to

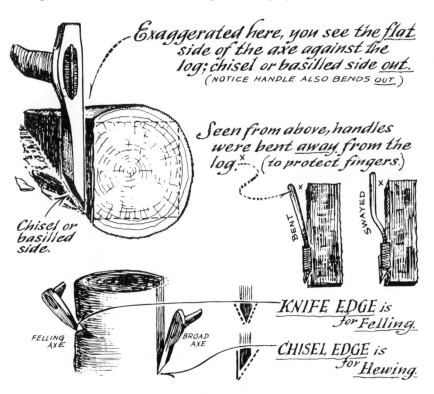

Exaggerated here, you see the flat side of the axe against the log; chisel or basilled side out.
(NOTICE HANDLE ALSO BENDS OUT)

Seen from above, handles were bent away from the log. (*to protect fingers.*)

BENT   SWAYED

Chisel or basilled side.

FELLING AXE   BROAD AXE

KNIFE EDGE is *for Felling.*

CHISEL EDGE is *for Hewing.*

FIGURE 9.   *Drawings by Eric Sloane showing the difference between a hewing axe and a felling axe, the former used for converting a tree trunk into a flat-sided piece of timber and the latter for cutting down the tree in the first place.* From A Museum of Early American Tools *by Eric Sloane. Copyright © 1964. Reprinted by permission.*

a ton, had to be laid on blocks and held in place by driving two-pronged iron "dogs" into the log and the block. The carpenter then produced the first flat surface by using his felling axe to make a line of parallel scores across the grain at regular intervals along the length of the log, guided by a chalk line Once the side was scored, he sliced away the pieces between the cuts with his heavy broad axe. Unlike the blade of the cutting axe, which was beveled on both sides to produce a knife edge, the broad axe blade was beveled on only one side, like a chisel. By keeping the unbeveled straight side of the blade next to the log, a skilled workman could produce a remarkably flat surface, marked only by the shallow remains of evenly spaced parallel score lines running across its

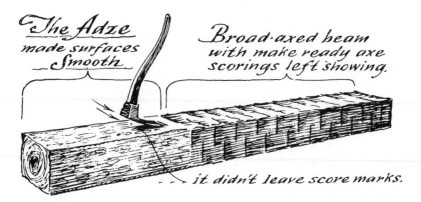

The Adze made surfaces Smooth

Broad·axed beam with make ready axe scorings left showing.

it didn't leave score marks.

FIGURE 10. *Drawing by Eric Sloane showing the design and use of a carpenter's adze. From* A Museum of Early American Tools *by Eric Sloane. Copyright © 1964. Reprinted by permission.*

breadth. Then the log had to be turned so the carpenter could repeat the process on the next side, and so on until he had fashioned a round log into a four-sided piece of timber.[23]

Hewing and sawing out the timbers was only the first step of the framing process. We do not know where Barker's men assembled the frame. It was not uncommon for frames of houses and even larger buildings to be assembled in carpenters' yards, even at some distance, and then transported to the site as disassembled timbers.[24] While this method would have had some advantages of convenience and security, there is the strong possibility, in the absence of evidence to the contrary, that the main work of putting the frame together took place during the summer of 1773 in the broad open space of the hilltop Wilton common. There was room enough there that clearing, digging the trenches, and preparing the foundation could have proceeded at the same time that the frame was being laid out close by.

The key to a solid frame was its joints. Some were simple, some very complex. All had to be carefully measured and "scribed," or marked out on the timber before cutting into it, either with a twin-bladed hatchet-like tool called a "twibel" or with auger and chisel.[25] Most consisted of some version or combination of the mortise and tenon, usually a chiseled opening on one stick that received the narrowed and shaped end of another, the two pieces

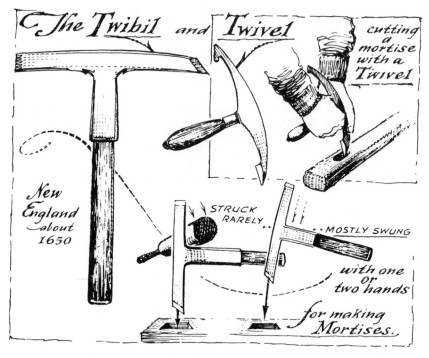

The Twibil *and* Twivel

cutting a mortise with a Twivel

New England about 1650

STRUCK RARELY

MOSTLY SWUNG

with one or two hands

for making Mortises.

FIGURE 11. *Drawing by Eric Sloane of the twibil ("twin bill") and the twivel, showing their use in cutting mortises. From* A Museum of Early American Tools *by Eric Sloane. Copyright © 1964. Reprinted by permission.*

held in place by a wooden pin that ran through both. Carpenters laid out the pieces of the entire frame on the ground, and then shaped both parts—or in some cases *all* parts—of the joint wherever timbers needed to be joined. Whereas the more standardized methods of the early nineteenth century could produce something like interchangeable parts, the Wilton workmen made joints essentially the same way their great-grandfathers had done it, by fitting each tenon to a particular mortise.

The joining of the pieces of a section of the frame, or "bent," was a relatively simple matter compared to preparing for the moment that the sides of the frame would be joined while being held upright, and especially when post, plate, tie beam, and the lower end of a rafter would have to meet at six points along each side of the building. That particular intersection called for an intricate combination of mortise and a special squared tenon called a "teazle," sawed rabbet joints, and augured holes with connecting pins, all carefully designed according to the vernacular methods of the day to create a compact and solid unit. The aim was to create the tightest possible joints, a matter of pride to the master builder. One such personage of the era, unless the poet working from communal memory made it up altogether, boasted "That every joint he ever framed / He knew would pinch a hair."[26]

The trees from which the twenty-seven-foot posts were hewn, if the normal practice was followed here, were placed upside down from their natural growing position in order to provide a broadened surface at the top, perhaps enhanced by producing a flare at the end during the hewing process, upon which the plate and its joined appendages could firmly rest. The frame contained other specialized joints as well, one type for the intersection of floor joists with sill, another for the intersection of purlins with rafters, and yet another to connect each of the four king posts with the apex of converging rafters at the top and a great tie beam, which it would hold in tension below. So that the raising crew would be able to fit the parts together properly, the carpenters used a chisel or knife to mark both pieces of each joint with the identical number in modified Roman numerals.[27]

The Wilton meetinghouse frame included certain features of the roof structure that were neither uncommon nor universal. One of the newspaper accounts about the raising refers to "another double pair of principals with a king post."[28] Thus we know that the building contained both "principal" and "common" rafters, that the principal rafters were doubled, and, from this and other sources, that the design used king posts, unlike the queen post method in the nearby Amherst meetinghouse that Barker was building at about the same time. The principal rafters were those that were joined at the foot to the plate, a tie beam, and a post, one of the main vertical supports of the building. Chances are there were six pairs of principals, since that was the usual number.[29] The intervening common rafters, smaller than the principals and often called "spars," were fitted into the plates at less crucial spots along the way. Their job was mainly to help support the horizontal roof boards rather than to play a role, as the principals

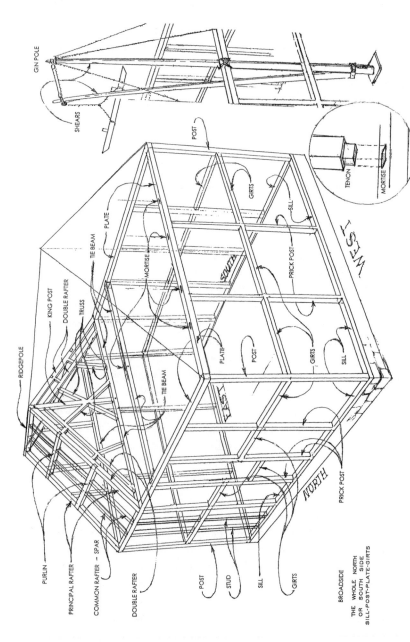

FIGURE 12.   *The parts of a meetinghouse frame. Drawing by John W. Hatch.*

did, in holding the building together. The reference to "double principals" indicates that each of principal rafters was supplemented by a second rafter running beneath and nearly parallel to it, anchored into the tie beam at the foot and into the king post a short distance below the peak. The rafter and king post assembly was strengthened by a system of cross bracing made of sawn timbers, the whole combination forming one of the building's principal roof trusses.[30] Each truss, in turn, was braced with sawn timbers to its adjoining ones.

By the time Ephraim Barker mustered his 120-man raising crew early on the morning of September 7, the carpenters had already laid atop the stone foundation the heavy sill pieces, joined at the corners of the building and fitted at intervals with heavy girders, supported by rocks beneath and running across the narrow dimension of the building to connect and stabilize the sixty-foot north and south sills. Chances are there were four such girders, one for each set of inside vertical posts. The girders, in turn, along with the end sills, were mortised to receive the floor joists, which would be oriented east and west, along the long dimension of the building. The joists or "sleepers" themselves, probably logs flattened on the upper side only, may also have been in place, and it is likely that the sleepers in turn were already laid either with temporary planks to form a flat working surface or with the permanent floor itself.[31]

There is no way of knowing exactly how Barker's men raised the meetinghouse walls. The frame of each of the side walls could have gone up in sections, or "bents," in which case, after the bents were raised and joined, the great timbers that formed the side plates would have needed to be lifted twenty-seven feet by some contrivance and fitted atop the joined bents to the upright posts, a difficult task at best. Most likely, however, judging from descriptions of two other New Hampshire raisings in the same era, the frame of each of the two side walls was assembled complete to form a "broadside," plate and all.[32] Barker may have used some kind of simple derricks, or "gin poles," to assist in raising the frame upright, just as some such device, along with block and tackle, was certainly used to lift tie beams and the components of roof trusses once the walls were standing.[33] In addition to six twenty-seven-foot posts, probably of oak, and the sixty-foot plate to which they were joined at fifteen-foot intervals, the posts of each broadside would have been further connected about halfway between top and bottom by smaller horizontal members called girts. The girts not only helped hold the posts parallel but would later serve to support an array of vertical studs, several of which would be deployed at intervals between the posts to provide bearings for the sheathing boards.

One particularly frustrating question, to be answered only by speculation and without great confidence, is whether the two long broadsides of the building were raised from the inside or from the outside. At the outset, that is, were the two assembled sides lying on the ground with the tops outward, or were one or both lying on the flatter and more solid floor, even though there was not room in the forty-five-foot width of the building for both assembled twenty-seven-foot high broadsides to lie absolutely flat if both were entirely within the sills? Was, perhaps, only one broadside assembled before the raisers went to work, and the other put together on the floor once the first was up? Or was the assembling and pinning of *both* broadsides part of the work of raising day? That would have resulted in a delay in the raising, an interval during which the available massed muscle power was not being fully employed. That one consideration, in fact, is what lends the most weight to a theory that the two broadsides were laid stretching outward from the foundation, the two forty-five-foot gable end wall bents perhaps also preassembled and lying on the floor to be raised from within.

On the other hand, my acquaintances who are experienced in putting up roughly comparable buildings unanimously stress the advantages of framing on a solid level surface. Not only is it easier to work on such a surface than on irregular ground, but with the timbers lying flat, there is a far better chance of achieving the necessary tight fit in every joint. Moreover, a broadside lying on the floor would have been level, or nearly so, with the sill into which the foot of each post had to be fitted, another advantage over doing the job from outside the foundation and sill, the top of which was perhaps a foot above the ground. For the purpose of the narrative that follows, and of the accompanying illustrations, it is that argument that has carried the day.[34]

Let us assume, therefore, that at least one of the two enormous broadsides was lying on the floor, the foot of each of its six posts touching the sill at the point that the tenoned end would fit into a mortise. The great beams that would be hoisted to form tie beams and trusses lay nearby, the joints matched and numbered and prepared for fitting once aloft. Now it was time for the job that only massed muscle power could do.

After the morning's first swallow of strengthening rum, dozens of men placed their brawny arms, toughened by daily labor in their own fields, at the top of the first dormant broadside and got their hands under the ten by ten-inch sixty-foot long plate, which by itself weighed between one thousand two hundred and one thousand three hundred pounds.[35] The master builder stood in some prominent place where he could be seen and heard by all, perhaps, as was sometimes the case, perched on the frame itself, upon which he would ride as it rose.[36] On his command, they began to lift. The mind's ear can easily discern the great choral shout-grunt at the instant the structure left the floor. Surviving accounts of comparable raisings include shouted commands and responses that fall strangely on modern ears but nevertheless have the ring of authenticity. One such account reports the litany, partly borrowed from the language of the sea, like this: "'Are you ready all?' 'Aye! aye!' 'Take hold all!' . . . 'Now, then!' . . . 'Heave away, my hearties!' . . . 'Now she rises!' . . . 'Heigh O! my hearties!'" And so on. Another, in verse form, quotes the master builder calling from his perch on a log, "'Now, All together; Right up with it.' / 'Up with it,' echoed round."[37] In some such way, Barker issued his commands, the huge plate inched off the ground, and the broadside began to move slowly upward.

The arms then kept working their way down the frame as powerful legs moved slowly in the direction of the foundation, raising the frame toward a vertical position as they moved. To keep the bottom of the frame from sliding outward during the process, a second crew, consisting of the strongest and most experienced workmen of all, wielded large iron bars at the foot of each post,

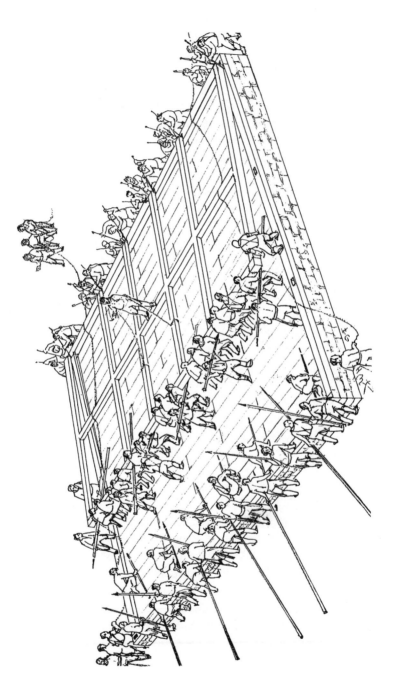

FIGURE 13. Conjectural view of the raising crew beginning to raise the south broadside of the Wilton meetinghouse. Ephraim Barker, the master builder, is issuing commands as he stands on the frame. The crew at the far right uses iron bars to keep the foot of the frame from sliding off the sill. The men at the far left, equipped with pike poles, are ready to move in when the broadside has been partly raised. Drawing by John W. Hatch.

straining against the lateral force of the raising crew that was marching slowly toward them and preparing to guide the post into its proper opening as the broadside became upright. When arms and legs alone were insufficient to stand this section of frame any higher, other workmen attacked with long iron-tipped pike poles, reaching as far toward the top as they could and gradually helping to push the frame upright until its tenoned feet were seated firmly in the mortises of the sill. As an aid to sheer muscle power, others may have been pulling on ropes attached to the top of the frame and running through the tackle blocks that were suspended from gin poles, which would later be used to hoist tie beams and rafters. The watching crowd cheered as temporary braces were quickly applied to hold the broadside in place, and after refreshing itself with another drop, the crew moved to the opposite side of the foundation to tackle the other long broadside and repeat the process, possibly after helping the joiners fit it together or, if it had already been assembled and was partly overhanging the sill until now, sliding it into position before the lifting began again. And so it went for the better part of a morning that had begun at six o'clock or earlier.[38]

At some time before noon, when ravenous appetites and thirsts were fed by the huge quantities of food and drink that the community provided, the latter at public expense, the wall frame and extra supports for the gallery inside the frame were in place and strengthened by both permanent and temporary diagonal bracing. Now it was time for more difficult tasks. First either four or six fifty-four-foot tie beams, depending upon whether the two that doubled as end plates had already gone up with their parts of the frame, had to be lifted twenty-seven feet to be put in place across the width of the building atop the side wall posts. The Wilton records contain no clue as to how this was accomplished, but when the town of Boxford, Massachusetts, built a meetinghouse in 1701, the voters appropriated money "for the geer and Ropes to Raies the meting houes" and even to pay a townsman, evidently the owner from whom the equipment was hired, to take the "Roopes and blockes" home again.[39] Unsurprisingly, therefore, the preeminent eighteenth-century lifting device was probably the block and tackle. Builders of the period were also familiar

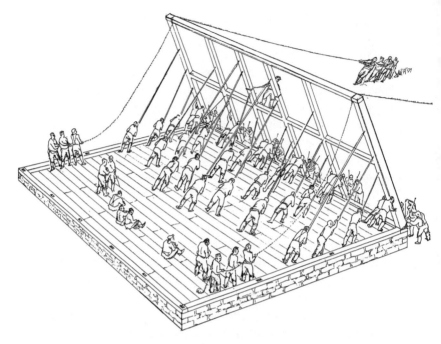

FIGURE 14. *Conjectural view of raising the south broadside, using pike poles and ropes, just before it becomes fully erect. Barker has maintained his perch on a girt. Drawing by John W. Hatch.*

with a simple form of derrick called a "shears" and knew how to build and use a windlass.[40] All of these devices, of course, were part of the European folk heritage, having been used on land and at sea for centuries, often for far more imposing projects—such as castles and cathedrals—than a New England meetinghouse.

If the tie beams were lifted by block and tackle, the gear had to be hung somehow above the level of the plate, which at that stage was the highest point on the structure itself. The builders, therefore, no doubt resorted to "gin poles," temporary single-member derricks fixed in place somewhere either on the frame or possibly just outside the building. The tackle could be rigged from the top of each pole and secured to the ends of the beams resting on the ground beneath. Manpower at this crucial moment might have been aided by windlass, or even by ox power.[41] The job of the tie beams was to counter the tendency of the structure to spread apart as the weight of roof and trusses bore down on the side plates, and thus were connected to the plates with joints designed to resist outward tension. The two tie beams at the gable ends of the building, like the side plates, were supported by posts. Each of the four intervening beams, on the other hand, had to be supported from above to keep it from sagging in the middle of its forty-five-foot span and perhaps breaking of its own weight. That was the main function of the four fifteen-foot king posts, each suspended from the joined principal rafters at the peak of the roof, its lower end mortised to penetrate entirely through the tie beam and be pinned beneath the beam to hold it in tension. The king posts also provided part of the elaborate system of bracing that stabilized each rafter truss. Obviously, to accommodate the penetrating tendon, the beam had to be fitted at its center with a rather large mortise extending entirely through it. Halfway along each of the four interior tie beams, in short, there was a good-sized hole. Because Ephraim Barker knew that this hole would have a weakening effect, he ordered each beam, once joined with the plates at the ends, to be supported in the center by a "shore," or temporary post — actually a twenty-seven-foot length of tree — until its associated rafter truss was in place and the king post securely mortised to it. What he may not have known is that one of the trees selected for this job may have been unsound. (It had fallen at either the wrong moment or in the wrong direction and had killed the man who was felling it, Isaac Russell.)[42]

It was now time to assemble and then to raise the six sets of doubled principal rafters, beginning at the east end of the building next to the road and moving along its length from one evenly spaced pair of opposed posts and connecting tie beam to the next.[43] This was the most difficult and hazardous part of the framing, as well as its culminating moment. It took a special combination of strength, agility, courage, and experience to be one of the fifty-two men Barker chose to climb with him to the top of the structure for this final task. Across the beams, each supported at the ends by side wall posts and in the middle by a temporary shore, the crew laid planks on which to assemble the prefitted and properly marked pieces of each truss, consisting in each case of the pair of double rafters, the king post, and various diagonal

braces. When they were all in place, king posts properly sus-
pending the beams beneath, there would be more braces connecting truss to truss and several sets of common rafters scattered
between the principals, the whole joined by the ridgepole and, on
each side of the roof, by one or more purlins, relatively light horizontal pieces running the length of the building across the rafters
between ridgepole and eaves. Installing some of these secondary
pieces of the roof frame, however, would be an easy task compared to the heavy lifting that was being done on September 7,
though no raising could be counted complete without the ceremonial toasting and alcoholic baptism of the ridge pole by some
acrobatic young man at the end of the day.[44] What was most important to accomplish in the nine allotted hours today were the
tasks that required the joint efforts of the great raising crew that
had gathered on Wilton common. Foremost among the remaining
ones was the raising of the principal rafters. One by one, trusses
weighing more than a ton when assembled on the staging planks,
their joints sometimes needing some extra shaving and some urging into place with axes, crowbars, and sledgehammers, were
raised to their vertical position by the clambering crew and anchored into place, their king posts securely fastened to the tie
beam so that the shore could be removed. By mid-afternoon, the
projected time for completion, fifty-three mostly young men, eager to get on with the celebration, were muscling either the third
or the fourth truss upright.

Disaster

❦ ❧

All on a Sudden a beam broak
it let down fifty three
full twenty seven feet they fell
a shocking sight to see

$\mathcal{A}$t a proud thirty years of age, John Bradford had been a commander of men. He had led the Amherst militia company, which now entitled him to the courtesy title of "Captain." He was also a substantial landowner. In 1771 he had bought 145 acres of land at the southern end of Lyndeborough and the next year added the entire adjoining farm lot, right next to the Wilton town line.[1] All this in addition to the lands he owned in Amherst, to which he would soon return. There is no evidence to prove it, but one must surmise that he knew through experience something about constructing and raising large buildings. He also knew, as he rode onto the Wilton common in the afternoon of that September 7, that something was wrong.

Sarah, his wife, had been ill that day, so the young captain was on the scene rather late. In fact it was about three in the afternoon. Perhaps already delayed because of concern over her health, the two had decided at length that he would do his neighborly duty to the people in Wilton, at least to the extent of taking part in the last, most difficult, stages. Sarah would ride along on the pillion behind his saddle, but would stay at the home of a Wilton friend to rest while her husband was at the building site. Now as Bradford rode up beside the raised frame of the body of the building and watched the fifty-three timber and rafter men struggling to place two of the great doubled rafters in place above one of the tie beams, his eye came to rest on Isaac Russell's tree. By eerie coincidence, the very same tree trunk that had killed Russell when he was felling it earlier in the year was now being used as a temporary central support for the tie beam from which the crew was now working. At least, that was the story that soon made its way around Wilton.[2] The two ends of the beam rested firmly on the building's plate timbers, but it was a stretch of forty-five feet across the width of the building, and the beam was weakened in the middle by the mortise that was intended to receive the tenon of the king post. Once the rafters above it had been put in place, and the king post suspended from the peak and joined with the beam at its center to hold it in position, the temporary support would be removed.

John Bradford saw what nobody else had noticed. The supporting tree trunk that served as the shore was not doing its job. Weakened either by worms or rot, it was beginning to crack and bend slightly under the immense weight from above. And to Bradford's horror, even more men, some of whom had been standing on planks to begin raising the rafter assembly, were now swarming toward the beam for the final push into position. At once Bradford leapt from his horse, ran to a ladder, climbed to where Ephraim Barker was directing the action aloft, and told him of the danger. Barker, exhilarated by the crew's success so far and possibly emboldened by some of the good rum punch being served below, reacted with scorn. "If you're afraid to work on this job," Barker said in effect, "go on home. We want no cowards here." Bradford, as angry at being called a coward as concerned about the safety of the crew, abruptly descended the ladder, mounted his horse, and headed off. Sarah, it seemed at this point, needed him more than the insolent Barker needed him.[3]

At the moment that this little drama was being played out, the mulatto man who had been entertaining the spectators with tricks of sleight-of-hand now turned to a gymnastic act he had taught himself. It consisted of "dancing on the edge of a bowl." We have been left in the dark as to the bowl's size, shape, and composition, but chances are it was a wooden bowl stood on edge, providing a rotating platform for the nimble-footed dancer. According to Colonel Reuben Kidder's slave Caesar, one of the many spectators who circled the performance, the dance ended abruptly when the bowl broke. The terrified dancer, identifying the incident as an omen, exclaimed that his dance had never before broken a bowl, "and there would be bloody work there soon."[4]

Moments later, as John Bradford rode slowly out of the clearing, looking anxiously back at the building site that he knew to be full of danger, the frame shuddered, scattering to safety the sixty or seventy workmen who were still on the ground watching their neighbors strain at the rafters. In an instant, there was a crash heard nearly a mile away. For another moment there was silence, and then a confusion of agonized sounds that seemed to Caesar just a single immense scream. A scream "that rung in his ears for years after."[5]

What Bradford had feared, and what the master builder had dismissed as old-maidish qualms, had finally, abruptly, come to pass. Isaac Russell's tree collapsed, and with it the weakened center of the beam that supported fifty-three straining men, either standing directly on the beam or on planks that rested partly on it. Down came the two halves of the immense broken beam, and down came the double pair of rafters with all the associated supporting members. Down came the planks, and the axes, sledgehammers, and great crowbars that the workmen had carried aloft. And down plunged the fifty-three workmen, twenty-seven feet to the plank-covered joists beneath, equivalent to a fall from the roof of a modern three-story house. Not a single one escaped injury.

The first to die was George Lancey, one of the sixteen Wilton men in the rafter crew. Whether his head struck the hard floor or whether he was crushed by a falling timber is not recorded, but he was killed outright. Reuben Stiles of Lyndeborough and Simeon Fletcher of New Ipswich succumbed next, either crushed or cut so severely that they bled to death within minutes. Two more Lyndeborough men, Joseph Severance and Timothy Carlton, survived only briefly, Severance until the next day and Carlton until the end of the week four days later.[6]

Only two specific injuries to the other forty-eight are recorded by name, William Spear's broken ribs and Simeon Wright's crushed ankle.[7] What happened to the rest, however, is clear enough. A newspaper account describes a scene of blood and brains, a stillness suddenly pierced by "shrieks and Groans," and "broken bones, terrible bruises or wounds from the axes." From

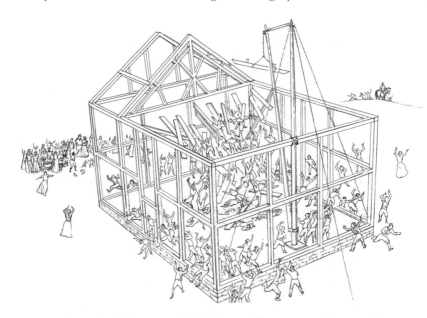

FIGURE 15.　*Artist's conception of the Wilton meetinghouse raising at the moment the tie beam gave way. In the center of the frame is the breaking tree trunk that was being used as a temporary shore for the beam while the rafters and king post were being put in place. The man on horseback at the upper right is John Bradford, who began to ride away from the scene after futilely warning builder Ephraim Barker of the danger. Drawing by John W. Hatch.*

another source we learn of fractures to shoulders, arms, and legs, and the earliest published reports from the scene assume several more fatalities than actually occurred.

Unfortunately for any attempt to reconstruct the scene in detail, the available sources do not describe what was surely, after a moment's stunned silence, an immediate rush by other workers and onlookers, including Captain Bradford who galloped back to the meetinghouse site, to aid the victims. We know nothing except what can be imagined of frantic efforts to remove the two halves of the great beam and the other timbers and planks from broken and bleeding bodies. We are not told by whom or by what means the victims were taken from the confused and jumbled mass of debris and humanity, or what possible means of first aid might have been administered on the scene. It is hard at this distance even to visualize the victims' long and painful ride on horseback or in a wagon from the Wilton common to nearly fifty widely scattered homes in eight separate communities. Were some of the injured, perhaps many, lodged for a time in some nearby houses, such as Mr. Livermore's parsonage or the home of John Cram, before making the trip home to other parts of Wilton, to Lyndeborough, to New Ipswich, to Temple, or to Mile Slip, Mason, New Concord, or Andover or Pepperrell, Massachusetts? We can only guess. Chances are that the master builder himself, whose home was still fifty miles away in Stratham, did not go there at all in the immediate aftermath of the tragedy. Then there were three dead bodies to be removed and tended to, the first three of what would prove to be five fatalities.

And what of all the others on the scene, those who were not among the fifty-three who fell? There were more than sixty other workmen who stood nearby, and an untold number of spectators and celebrators from Wilton and adjoining towns, probably numbering in the hundreds. What, especially, of the parents, the brothers and sisters, the wives, the children, and the one "maiden lover," as one version of the ballad calls her, of the victims? Certainly they shared the sensation of immediate horror with all their neighbors who watched, but theirs was a special anguish; no doubt they made their own contribution to the single great scream that lived in Caesar's memory.

The news traveled rapidly. In Wilton, so many of the community were eyewitnesses that it was not long before every household knew. Who, we wonder, had to bear the news to Elizabeth Lancey, pregnant and at home with the two surviving children of the three that she and George had brought into the world? To the adjoining towns of Lyndeborough, New Ipswich, and Temple, all heavy contributors to the work force, uninjured workmen and spectators returned to tell their scattered neighbors. We can guess that all of these communities were fully informed by nightfall. From New Ipswich, which gave up one dead and eight injured, an unnamed correspondent wrote to the *Massachusetts Gazette*: "And as they were men picked up from that [Wilton] and neighboring towns, and many of them heads of families, the news of their catastrophe filled those places with weeping, lamentation and woe."

Within less than six days, the news had reached Boston in the
form of a "letter from New-Ipswich." It is impossible to tell
whether the author was an eyewitness or whether his quickly
composed account came from hearsay. It is, however, remarkably
full of details, providing one of the best sources for our attempt to
reconstruct the event. It could not have left New Ipswich before
Saturday, the day of Timothy Carlton's death, which the letter
faithfully records. Because of its more southern location, next to
the border and served by the beginnings of an east-west road that
bypassed Wilton, the journey from New Ipswich to the metropo-
lis was a bit easier and quicker than it would have been from any
of the other three most seriously affected communities. One
could ride east on a road just north of the Massachusetts border,
turn south at the Merrimack River, cross the border at Dunstable,
and finally pick up the same road through Concord and Lexington
over which, a bare nineteen months in the future, several British
columns would be marching in the opposite direction not knowing they were about to change the history of the empire. There
was as yet no postrider, so whoever made the two-day seventy-
mile journey either did so expressly to deliver the letter or was on
a business errand to Boston.[8] The record bears no clue as to who
might have written it, but a good guess might be the minister of
New Ipswich, the Reverend Stephen Farrar. Not only would
Mr. Farrar have had the requisite command of the written language and the Boston connections to get a letter into the *Gazette*,
but the scriptural passages and moral lesson with which the letter
ends suggest, but do not prove, clerical authorship.

Here is what Richard Draper's *Massachusetts Gazette and
Weekly News-Letter* printed in the number for Monday, September 13, the printer having set it in type the previous Saturday after
the arrival of the rider from New Ipswich or on the Monday morning of publication:

Extract of a letter from New-Ipswich, Sept. 13, 1773.
    Last Tuesday the most melancholy accident of the kind, happened at
Wilton, in New-Hampshire Government, that perhaps has been known in
the Country: A large company was collected there to raise a Meeting-House,
and they got up the body of it, the beams and joists, and on these had a large
quantity of boards for the more immediate convenient standing; they had
also raised part of the roof, in doing which they had occasion for a number

of crowbars and axes, which rested on the building while the people got together, and were in the act of raising another double pair of principals with a king-post, when on a sudden the beam broke at the mortice in the middle, by which upwards of fifty persons fell to the bottom of the house, with the timber, bars, axes, &c. and exhibited a scene to the astonished spectators around the house (for there were no persons in the bottom of it, all having withdrawn through fear of what might happen) which cannot be described; and could only be equalled by the blood and brains, shrieks and groans of the dead and wounded, which were immediately seen and heard. Three were killed outright; another survived but a short time, and several others have since died of their wounds. Of fifty-three that fell, not one escaped without broken bones, terrible bruises or wounds from the axes, &c. And as they were men picked up from that and neighboring towns, and many of them heads of families, the news of their catastrophe filled those places with weeping, lamentation and woe, and may fully mind us that "Man knoweth not his time," but "at such an hour as we think not the son of Man cometh," and it therefore concerns us to be always ready.[9]

To the letter is attached a list of casualties, organized by town. Lancey (spelled Laney), Fletcher, and Stiles are listed accurately as "killed instantly." Five are described as "mortally wounded," including Severance ("Suerance") and Carlton ("Calton"), both reported to have since died, Severance after one day and Carlton after four. Francis Putnam and Ebenezer Coster of Wilton were "both expected to be dead before this Time," and Benjamin Jones of Lyndeborough was "supposed to be since dead." All three, though obviously injured desperately, eventually recovered. The list contains the names of thirty-seven other victims, all listed as "wounded."[10]

Boston, still the publishing capital of the British American colonies, had four other newspapers besides the *Gazette*, three of which published on Mondays. The September 13 number of the *Boston Gazette and Country Journal* cannot be found. Both the *Boston Evening-Post* and the *Massachusetts Gazette and Boston Post-Boy and Advertiser* carried accounts of the Wilton tragedy that day, though much shorter than the other *Massachusetts Gazette*'s. Since there are only slight variations in wording between the two, they could have come from the same source, different from the "letter from New-Ipswich" in Draper's *Gazette*, though the *Post-Boy* apparently garbled the story on its first try. The *Evening-Post* reported, "We learn from Wilton, in New Hampshire, that on Tuesday last, as a great number of Persons were assisting in raising the Frame of a new Meeting House in that Town, one of the large beams accidentally fell, by which means four of the Men were instantly killed, and 49 wounded, two or three of whom are since dead, and it was tho't several others of them could not recover." Though much less detailed than the "letter from New Ipswich," this account was reasonably accurate. The *Post-Boy's* brief account, consisting like the *Evening-Post's* of just one complex sentence, used some of the same wording but attributed the accident to the collapse of a king post, stated incorrectly that the "greatest Part of the Frame fell to the Ground," reported seven fatalities, and dropped a crucial line of type. On Thursday the sixteenth, the semiweekly paper corrected most of its errors simply by copying the *Evening-Post's* version. On the same day, the *Massachusetts Gazette and Boston Weekly News-Letter* also copied that version. From that point on, the *Massachusetts Gazette's* "long" version in the letter from New Ipswich and the *Evening-Post's* "short" version provided the two main sources, through the accepted practice of mutual copying, for the spread of news of the meetinghouse tragedy. There were, however, two other early printed reports. Boston's fifth newspaper, Isaiah Thomas's two-year-old *Massachusetts Spy*, like the *Massachusetts Gazette*, came out on Thursday. On the sixteenth, while the *Post-Boy* and *Gazette* were reprinting what was fast becoming the standard "short" version, the *Spy* came out with a more up-to-date account, not quite as detailed as the "Letter from New-Ipswich" but more accurate than it and the short version in its enumeration of casualties and adding a detail at the end that had not yet been reported:

On Tuesday se'ennight, as a great number of people were assisting in raising the frame of a new meeting house in Wilton New-Hampshire, one of the large beams accidentally gave way, when the greatest part of the frame, with fifty-three persons that were upon it, fell to the ground, by which unhappy event, three men were instantly killed, and fifty wounded, two of whom have since died of their wounds, and four more are thought to be past recovery. This accident has put by the raising for the present.

In New Hampshire, the province where it all happened, Daniel Fowle's *New-Hampshire Gazette* of Portsmouth came out on Friday. In language distinctly different from any of the Boston accounts, furnishing a few important new details but exaggerating the numbers both of fatalities and of those who fell, Fowle printed the following account on September 17:

The 7th Instant, being the Day appointed for raising a new Meeting-House in Wilton, 60 by 45 Feet, 27 Feet Post; 120 Men were pitch'd upon to perform the Business, which they design'd to accomplish in nine Hours, and had almost completed the same by three o'Clock in the Afternoon, when a most shocking and melancholly Accident happened in the following Manner, viz. The Shore which was put under the middle Beam to strengthen it, while the King Post and Spars of the Roof were fixing, gave Way, and 60 Men fell, when three were instantly kill'd, and a fourth soon after died of his Wounds. Above 50 of the 60 are kill'd and wounded, some with broken Legs, Arms, &c. and 'tis expected a Number more will not live.

Since the foregoing Account we hear five more are dead.

We expected before the publication of this Paper, a more particular Account of the above Accident, would have been sent, with the Names of the kill'd and wounded, but it being neglected, can give no better than the foregoing.

The following is said to be the Names of those that died first, Coaster, Chandler, Caldwell, two Millikens, Wiggins, and Hutchison.

Fowle's account gives every indication of having been composed by the printer himself, probably on the basis of two or more separate word-of-mouth reports by travelers to Portsmouth during the previous week. The type was set in installments, at least two, perhaps three or four. The printer expresses frustration at not being able to complete the story to his satisfaction. There was ample time, given the post schedule, for him to have received all three of the previous Monday's Boston newspapers, but he obviously wanted to provide his own more complete account for his New Hampshire readers. One result of his determination was that, despite the inclusion of some useful details missing from the Boston reports, including the precise cause of the accident, not a single fatality was recorded accurately.

In the decades before there was any conscious attempt in America toward the professionalization of journalism, and a very long time before the specialized occupations of "reporter" and "editor" had occurred to anyone, the printed word, especially in the ephemeral world of the weekly newspaper, was often a simple extension of the spoken word. The phrase "we hear" that introduces many locally generated news reports of the day should be taken literally. What the printer heard was no different in accu-

racy or quality from what anyone else might hear; the act of printing simply created a larger and more widespread audience for
what was already being circulated in more limited circles by word
of mouth. One can easily imagine the hasty, somewhat hysterical
reports of the events on Wilton common, complete with erroneous early details, that made their way from house to house in
the hours after the disaster. Unlike the written letter from New
Ipswich, a deliberate and largely successful attempt to tell the
story faithfully with the express intention of having it published,
the rumor mill operated, as it still does, without definite boundaries or verified information. No one from Wilton or the surrounding towns would have traveled any distance during the week
after the accident, as apparently at least a few did to Portsmouth,
without bearing with them whatever they had seen or heard about
this sensational event. Clearly, not everyone had heard precisely
the same story. In sharing as much as he could piece together of
that story with his readers, Daniel Fowle made do with what he
had. On the next Friday, apparently having given up hope of getting better information directly from the scene and with the news
now grown cold even by eighteenth-century standards, Fowle
copied the "Excerpt from the letter from New-Ipswich," complete
with the casualty list, from the *Massachusetts Gazette*.[11]

The day before the *New-Hampshire Gazette* printed its first
tentative account, the *Boston Post-Boy*, then published twice a
week, had supplemented its Monday report by copying the
equally short but more accurate version in Monday's *Evening-Post*
in its Thursday number.[12] The same report appeared in Friday's
Connecticut Gazette in New London and in Saturday's *Providence
Gazette*. The next Monday, the *Evening-Post*, having already furnished what was now becoming the standard and presumed authoritative "short" version of the story, rounded out the record by
copying the *Massachusetts Gazette*'s letter from New Ipswich,
omitting the list of casualties.[13]

During the next week and a half, the news, having now traveled
outside New England by the postal transmission of the Boston
prints, was considered significant enough to appear in one newspaper in New York and two in Philadelphia. Both Philadelphia
newspapers, evidently by careless typesetting in each case, gave

the wrong date of the accident. In reprinting the *Boston Evening-Post*'s "short" version on September 22, the *Pennsylvania Journal* included it in a list of items mistakenly headed "Boston, August [rather than September] 13." A week later, the *Pennsylvania Gazette* copied the *Massachusetts Spy* account under the correct dateline of Boston, September 16 (the day the *Spy* published it), but somehow substituted "Thursday se'ennight" for "Tuesday se'ennight," thus misdating the accident by two days. The story does not appear to have been picked up by any printer south of Philadelphia.[14] On Monday, September 27, the *Boston Gazette and Country Journal* finally ran the letter from New Ispwich, a full two weeks after it had first appeared, adding eleven names from Lyndeborough to provide a more complete list of casualties.

News of the terrible accident, therefore, made its way from Wilton to Philadelphia and points between by all three possible modes, or "cultures," of communication: by word of mouth, by the relatively more formal and painstaking handwritten letter from New Ipswich, and by print, which, with its multiple copies, its link with the postal service, and the practice of mutual copying, was an especially powerful engine of transmission. The spread of the news, however, was neither the most lasting nor, to the communities involved, the most significant response to the meeting-house tragedy. In due time, perhaps very soon, someone wrote a ballad.

Before considering that important response, we need to look more closely at the victims of the tragedy.

The Victims

❧ ❧

It would pierce the hardest heart to hear
the bitter Cries and grones
of them that in the ruins Lay
with wounds and broaken bones

Some lay with broken sholder bones,
and some with broken arms,
Others with broken legs and thies
and divers other harms

Many lay bleeding on the ground
all barth'd in crimson gore
Crying dear Jesus mighty to save
thy mercy we implore

The modern reader may wonder, at first glance, whether the poet was indulging in a bit of hyperbole. As melodramatic as these lines certainly are by our own standards, however, they scarcely embellish (the exact words of the prayer to dear Jesus possibly excepted) what witnesses actually saw and heard. Far from embellishing, in fact, the poet took advantage of at least some separation from the event to correct some earlier impressions. While the ballad faithfully records the actual sequence of the five deaths caused by the accident, the report published ten days later by the *New-Hampshire Gazette* gives the surnames of seven "who died first," and assumes that "'a Number more will not live." The casualty list printed by the *Massachusetts Gazette* on September 13, otherwise reasonably accurate though not quite complete, includes under the heading "mortally wounded" the names of five victims who in fact survived. The ballad's description of the various injuries is fully consistent with all the accounts from the scene.

George Lancey of Wilton, his wife Elizabeth six months pregnant with their fourth child, died at once. Within minutes, the accident had also claimed the lives of two more. One was Reuben Stiles of Lyndeborough, the twenty-four-year-old unmarried son of Samuel Stiles and his wife Phebe, a member of the extensive Cram clan. The other was Simeon Fletcher of New Ipswich. Later that year Simeon's widow Rachel appeared on the town's tax list, and since the New Ipswich town history mentions descendants, there must have been one or more Fletcher children at the time of the accident. By the end of the week, two more Lyndeborough men were dead. Joseph Severance died the day afterward, on Wednesday, and Timothy Carlton, whose younger brother David was also injured, succumbed four days later, on Saturday.[1]

As to specific injuries resulting from the fall, the ballad's listing seems to follow fairly closely the presumably eyewitness account first published in the *Massachusetts Gazette*, suggesting in fact that it was this source upon which the strictly reportorial portions of the ballad may have been based. The letter comments on "a scene to the astonished spectators . . . which cannot be described; and could only be equalled by the blood and brains, shrieks and groans of the dead and wounded, which were immediately seen and heard. . . . Of fifty-three that fell, not one escaped without broken bones, terrible bruises or wounds from the axes."[2] Reports of exact injuries to specific individuals are hard to find. The historians of New Ipswich do mention William Spear's broken ribs and record that he was "maimed for life," and add a macabre twist to the tragic tale of Simeon Wright, whose ankle was "crushed by the falling timbers." Thirteen years later, having recovered the use of the ankle, Wright bled to death after accidently cutting the same one with an axe, apparently reopening the old wound.[3] Francis Putnam and Ebenezer Coster of Wilton and Benjamin Jones of Lyndeborough were among those that the *Massachusetts Gazette* listed as "mortally wounded," so one can only presume that the injuries to these three were more severe than those to the other forty-eight survivors. Evidently a number of the victims suffered broken bones; we know of William Spear's ribs, and the ballad, though not the report, specifies shoulders, arms, legs, and

thighs. Any of these fractures could have resulted simply from hit-
ting the flooring or by being struck by falling timber. The other
main category of casualty was cutting injuries, apparently caused
largely by dozens of plummeting axes.

Of the fifty-three known casualties, thirty were either Wilton
or Lyndeborough men, and another nine were from New Ipswich.
Temple contributed six, Mile-Slip (later part of Milford) two. Two
more had come up from Andover, Massachusetts, source of much
of Wilton's immigration in the previous decade, to help their relatives and former neighbors with the raising. There was one victim
each from nearby Mason just north of the Massachusetts border
and Pepperrell just south of it, one from more distant New Concord (later Washington, New Hampshire), and one, the master
builder Ephraim Barker, from Stratham, on the New Hampshire
coast about fifty miles to the east.

Of all the communities that contributed to the raising, it was
Lyndeborough that suffered the greatest loss. Wilton's sixteen casualties outnumbered Lyndeborough's fourteen, but that is far
from the whole story. Not only did Lyndeborough give up three
lives compared to one each from Wilton and New Ipswich, but
Lyndeborough's total population was somewhat smaller than
Wilton's. Thus the ratio of killed and injured to population,
though certainly comparable, was slightly higher: 3.2 percent of
the whole population and 13 percent of adult males as compared
with 2.8 percent of the population and 13 percent of adult males
in Wilton. The nine casualties from New Ipswich, whose population was more than twice that of Lyndeborough's, constituted
about 1 percent of that town's inhabitants and 5.3 percent of
its adult males. Six of the victims were from Temple, which with
418 inhabitants in 1773 was even smaller than Lyndeborough. Its
casualties were 1.4 percent of the population and 6.6 percent of
Temple's adult males.[4] In the case of Wilton or Lyndeborough, it
was as if one of today's small New England towns of perhaps ten
thousand were to experience a catastrophe—maybe a great fire or
explosion or the collapse of a snow-weighted roof in a crowded
public building—in which, while the whole town looked on,
three hundred people were injured and, to apply Lyndeborough's
experience, more than sixty of them were to die. It would be hard

to imagine a family in such a community that would not be touched in some way by the tragedy. How much more the case in these eighteenth-century New Hampshire communities whose life in its very essence consisted of frequent, often intimate, inter- action among neighbors, many of whom were kin. Certainly the impact especially on those two adjoining towns, closely con- nected by familial ties and overlapping origins, was grave.

Whether the fifty-three men who had climbed to the top of the frame to do the dangerous work of installing beams, king posts, and rafters were representative of the 120-man raising crew as a whole, we cannot know. Certainly some generalizations, such as the extent of relationships among the workers and distribution among neighboring communities, can safely be applied across the board. Others, such as age and family status, perhaps ought not to be so applied, since common sense suggests that as a group the victims must have been selected, perhaps self-selected, on the basis of youth, strength, or experience compared to the crew at large.

Among them, the available sources provide the names of all fifty-three killed or injured.[5] Not surprisingly, many of the vic- tims, even those from across town and even province boundaries, were related—a pattern we should be likely to find if we had the whole list of workmen as well.

No fewer than four of the fifty-three bore the family name of Blanchard, a conspicuous name in Wilton even though all four Blanchard victims came from elsewhere. No doubt several Wilton Blanchards, whose origins were in Andover, were part of the rais- ing crew. Three more were members of the large Wilton family of Putnam, which did not come from Andover, but had early settled that part of Salem Canada that later became the northern part of Wilton. Twenty-five-year-old Francis Putnam was so badly in- jured that he was listed as "mortally wounded" in the first account of the accident, though he later recovered. His father and mother, Nathaniel and Abigail, had been among those who had come to town from Danvers soon after the first settlement. Francis's first cousins, the brothers Joseph and Archelaus Putnam, were also in- jured. Their father Jacob, Nathaniel's brother, who at sixty-two was the patriarch of Wilton as well as its first settler, had served as a selectman in 1763. Joseph and Archelaus were among eleven children of Jacob and Susannah Putnam, the first two of whom had been born in Danvers before their parents settled in what became Wilton. The eldest, Sarah, was the wife of Jonathan Cram, a four-time town treasurer. Perhaps some of the other six brothers were also part of the crew, since the youngest, Peter, was already seventeen—he would die a soldier's death near Ticonderoga less than three years later. Archelaus, probably still unmarried though he would be twenty-four in another month, lived at his father's homestead, which he would eventually inherit.[6] Joseph, on the other hand, at twenty-nine a well established family man, farmer, and mill owner, had built his house and mill in the extreme northwestern corner of Wilton, just west of the parental farm, in the range of lots that in 1768 became a part of the new town of Temple. He and his wife Miriam already had five children ranging from three to nine, and would add five more to their family in the years to come.

Samuel and Alexander Milliken, both of Wilton, twenty-one and eighteen respectively, were among the five unmarried sons of the senior Alexander Milliken, an illiterate and possibly outlaw immigrant from Ireland who with his wife Mary had become an early settler of southern Salem Canada, not long after the Putnams. Samuel's twin brother William was likely part of the raising crew as well, possibly along with John, sixteen. The youngest brother Robert, at thirteen, would certainly not have been given much of a role in this dangerous business, if any, though we can well imagine that he was very much on the scene.[7]

Oliver and Fifield Holt were first cousins, both members of an extensive clan originating in Andover whose farms were located mainly in the area just south of the Wilton meetinghouse. Elizabeth, the wife of Isaac Frye, another of the injured who had come from Andover as part of a large family and lived in southern Wilton, was a cousin of the Holts. Jonathan Chamberlain and Uriah Cram, both of Lyndeborough, must have been relatives, since Uriah's mother was a Chamberlain, but the exact connection is unclear. So is the relationship between Simeon Fletcher of New Ipswich, one of the fatalities, and his fellow townsman Francis Fletcher, but there must have been one. The two men were not brothers, since according to a record in a family Bible, Simeon was one of eleven siblings, none of them named Francis.[8]

To name these sixteen of the fifty-three accident victims who were closely related to other victims is to suggest the degree of interrelatedness that was likely a feature of the work force as a whole. We have already noted potential members of the crew from the Putnam and Milliken families, for example. The Holts could have furnished others, and John Cram, Jr., to name another victim who was part of a large and prominent Wilton and Lyndeborough family, had four brothers in town who were over eighteen.

Not surprisingly, given the nature of the job and the fact that the towns that furnished the bulk of the work force were young communities with preponderantly young populations, the victims also tended to be rather young men. It is possible to determine the ages of twenty-one of the forty-five victims who came from the four adjoining towns that were the largest contributors to the work force—Wilton, Lyndeborough, New Ipswich, and Temple. Of those, the oldest, at forty-six, was William Spear of New Ipswich, one of the more severely injured;[9] the youngest was eighteen-year-old Samuel Milliken, one of the Milliken brothers from Wilton. The average age was twenty-nine, but there were variations among communities. Ten of the Wilton victims averaged twenty-seven, four of the Lyndeborough victims twenty-four, four New Ipswich victims thirty-eight, and three of the Temple victims thirty. We can approximate the ages of three others whose exact ages are not known: William Clary of New Ipswich was probably in his early forties, Joshua Foster of Temple between thirty-six and forty, and Stephen Saunders of Temple somewhere in his 20s.[10] Why it was that the New Ipswich delegation on the whole was considerably older than those of the three other towns, whose victims averaged twenty-seven, remains a puzzle; the settlement and incorporation of New Ipswich was roughly contemporaneous with that of the surrounding towns, though it had grown faster and thus, with a population of 882, was considerably larger than the other three.

The relative maturity of the New Ipswich victims compared to those from other places complicates the interpretation of one other piece of available data, namely the New Ipswich tax list of 1774. All of the eight New Ipswich victims on the list, including Simeon Fletcher's widow Rachel, were in the upper half of the town's taxpayers for the year after the accident, and all paid well above the average tax. Of the New Ipswich injured, only Elijah Flagg is unlisted. The remaining eight New Ipswich victims paid, on the average, one pound and five shillings in 1774, compared with the average for all the town's 215 taxpayers of seventeen shillings, eleven pence. Four of the eight were in the upper fifth of the tax list, the other four in the second fifth. Joseph Tucker, who paid one pound, seventeen shillings, and ten pence, was the eighteenth highest taxpayer in New Ipswich. Simeon Wright, seventy-sixth on the list, was the only one of the eight who paid less than a pound, but at nineteen shillings sixpence only barely. His tax, the lowest paid by any of the victims, was almost seven shillings above the town median of twelve shillings ten pence. Rachel Fletcher, widow of New Ipswich's one fatality, was thirty-ninth on the list at one pound, seven shillings, and sixpence. None of the meetinghouse victims was among the very highest taxpayers, since four on the list were in the three- or four-pound range and twelve others paid over two pounds. The town's highest taxpayer in 1774, at four pounds, seven shillings, and three pence, was Colonel Reuben Kidder, the founder and leading citizen of New Ipswich and a county justice of the peace, who shared with several of his fellow townsmen a connection with the Wilton meetinghouse raising, at least an indirect one. Not only was he the uncle of Elizabeth Kidder Livermore, wife of the Wilton minister, but he was the owner of "Old Caesar," the black slave who witnessed the scene and related a superstition-laced account of the tragedy for years thereafter. The presence in Wilton of Caesar, who often drove his master around in the only carriage in New Ipswich, raises the strong possibility that the fifty-year-old colonel was on the scene himself, perhaps even as a member of the raising crew.[11]

Thus the eight taxpaying New Ipswich victims were all a notch or two below the propertied elite of their town, but they were all among the town's more prosperous citizens. That men of this status should have been involved in the most dangerous and physically demanding phases of a neighboring town's meetinghouse raising is to modern eyes a fascinating disclosure. Among the possible motives for their participation, to the apparent exclusion of their smaller propertied fellow townsmen, was a sense of obligation. As a matter of course, these would have been among those most involved in financing and building a new meetinghouse in their own town in 1767, including the recruiting of helpers from Wilton and other adjoining towns. John Dutton, one of the victims, had been an early member of the building committee for that project.[12] Reflecting on the courage, strength, skill, and practical intelligence that the beam-and-rafter detail was called upon to exercise, one might even speculate that it was precisely these qualities, brought to bear upon the improvement and successful operation of a family farm, that had resulted in a better-than-average increase in their property and thus a relatively high position on the tax list. This may attest, in other words, to a much more direct correlation in these young communities between physical competence and economic success than we expect to find in our postindustrial age. Certainly, their involvement in that phase of the job, and the possible participation in the raising by their towns' richest and most respected citizen, attests to an ethos that did not distinguish between "gentility" and manual labor. Or if such a distinction was assumed, these communities by their own self-perception lacked, with the exception of the ministers and perhaps Colonel Kidder, a gentry. Difficult, dangerous, sweaty physical labor was not inappropriate for anyone, especially when engaged in a communal effort for a public purpose.

But was the New Ipswich contingent representative of the victims as a whole? Would comparable tax lists, if they were available, suggest similar conclusions for Wilton, Lyndeborough, and Temple? Based on the obvious similarities among the four principal communities involved, one is tempted to answer "yes." What prevents an easy leap to such an answer is the matter of age. As we have seen, the average age of the New Ipswich victims was nine years higher than the average age of the victims as a whole, far higher than that in any of the three adjoining towns. In societies such as these, the accumulation of taxable wealth, mainly in the form of property improvements, took time. Thus we would expect a man of forty to possess greater taxable wealth than a man of twenty-five, other factors being approximately equal. Of course, other things were not always equal. Joseph Tucker, for example, who was the biggest taxpayer of any of the New Ipswich victims, had inherited substantial property from his father, one of the earliest settlers of the town, who had died in 1769.[13] We do not know Tucker's age, but his wife Martha was only twenty-two when she died the same year as the Wilton tragedy. Thus Tucker's age and comparative wealth apparently do not correlate. Both William Spear and William Clary, in their forties the two oldest of the New Ipswich victims, were in the second rather than the first fifth of the tax list. The age of the New Ipswich victim who paid the lowest taxes, John Dutton, is unknown. These anomalies help dull our suspicion that the relatively high property standing of the eight New Ipswich victims within their own community had something to do with age, but they do not remove it altogether. Lacking the necessary records for the other three towns, we cannot know whether the New Ipswich findings about property apply across the board. To answer the question with what would seem to be a common-sense "yes" would entail the risk, though perhaps only a small risk, of being wrong.

It was not only the victims who suffered, but their families as well. This was particularly true, of course, in the case of at least two of the dead men who left young widows and children. In Wilton, George Lancey's wife, Elizabeth, sixth months pregnant, was left in charge of a son and a daughter, ages seven and a year and a half; the shock of her husband's instant death was compounded by the sad memory of the infant death, five years earlier, of their son, William. In New Ipswich, Simeon Fletcher left his wife Rachael and at least one child, probably more.[14] The anguish of two Lyndeborough families, though not perhaps the economic trauma, must have been equally severe. Samuel and Phebe Stiles lost their twenty-four-year-old son Reuben, and Jeremiah and Eunice Carlton their son Timothy; the Carltons also had to confront the injuries to Timothy's younger brother David, who survived the meetinghouse tragedy only to die at Bunker Hill a year and nine months later. All these three young victims were apparently living under their parents' roofs at the time of the accident.[15] The family status of the fifth fatality, Joseph Severance, is unknown. Some of the more doleful and sentimental verses of the ballad aim at provoking empathy for the mourning of widows, fathers, mothers, brothers and sisters, and children. The printed 1818 version adds "One maiden lover" to the list of bereaved.

Of the fifty-three dead and injured, twenty-one are known to have been married. One, the master builder Ephraim Barker, was a widower. Three of the victims, the two Lyndeborough fatalities, Reuben Stiles and Timothy Carlton, and their fellow townsman Uriah Cram, are known to have been unmarried. The Milliken brothers and Archelaus Putnam, all of Wilton, were probably single as well. That leaves twenty-six of undetermined marital status, but it is a reasonable guess that like the eighty-one percent of those whose marital status is known, a substantial majority of the twenty-six were married men.

The twenty married men and their wives and the one widower had among them forty-seven children and were expecting three more, an average of slightly more than two per family. Isaac Brewer of Temple had no children as yet, nor did Fifield Holt of Wilton or the seriously injured Benjamin Jones of Lyndeborough, though both were expectant fathers. A few, however, already had large families. There were five children in each of the households of Joseph and Miriam Putnam of Wilton, Joshua and Lydia Foster of Temple, and the forty-six-year-old William Spear and his wife of New Ipswich.

Along with most of their generation in this part of British America, the young injured survivors of the Wilton tragedy would overwhelmingly support the rebellion in the years just ahead. Not only did many of them formally attest their attachment to the Revolutionary cause (and only a small handful refused), but a re-markable number, in view of the presumed severity of the in-juries, recovered sufficiently to do active service in some phase of the war.

In Wilton, eight of the fifteen surviving casualties signed New Hampshire's Association Test of 1776, by which they promised to defend America against the hostile British. One survivor, Joseph Putnam, was one of the two defiant Wilton men who refused to sign.[16] Some of those whose names are missing from the Association Test were among the twenty-six Wilton men who were out of town on military service, thus expressing their attachment to the Revolutionary cause in another way.[17] Francis Putnam, a sergeant in Wilton's company of minutemen, and Isaac Frye, regimental quartermaster of one of New Hampshire's two militia regiments, had both fought at Bunker Hill along with thirty-six other Wilton men the previous June.[18] Neither signed the Association Test, obviously only because they lacked the opportunity to do so. Frye must have served continuously through much of the war, since he was subsequently commissioned as a captain in one of the three New Hampshire regiments that became attached to the Continental Army. Fifield Holt, who did sign the Test, was among the reinforcements who joined the siege of Boston in December 1775; his cousin Oliver Holt was away on the unsuccessful campaign against Canada when the document was being circulated for signatures.[19]

In all, eighteen of the forty-five surviving victims from New Hampshire—three were from Andover or Pepperell, Massachusetts—signed the Association Test, and of the forty-eight survivors, at least seventeen served actively in some phase of the Revolutionary conflict. At least one, David Carlton of Lyndeborough, lost his life in the war. Joshua Chandler was exempted from military service because of his essential duties as foreman of the Andover powder mill.[20]

Almost certainly, others of the surviving victims were made incapable of military service because of their injuries from the meetinghouse. We know, for example, of Simeon Wright's crushed ankle; William Spear, another New Ipswich casualty, was reported to be "maimed for life." The absence of more specific information about injuries to individuals is frustrating, but it is clear that some were very serious, especially among the five survivors listed originally as "mortally wounded"—though one of those was Wilton's Sergeant Francis Putnam. At least eighteen, however, recovered sufficiently to take part in the war.

Let us now attempt a composite portrait. A representative member of that special detachment of the raising crew that ascended the frame to put beams and rafters in place would have been a strong young man of twenty-nine or thirty, perhaps of some proven experience in framing a building. He would have come to the raising from one of the four adjoining towns of Wilton, Lynde-borough, Temple, or New Ipswich, to which he would have moved from Massachusetts as a boy with his parents. He would have had a wife in her twenties and one, two, or three very young children at home. If the New Ipswich findings have any validity at all as a generalization for the whole crew—but that assumption is subject to question—our representative young man, while not among the very wealthiest of his fellow townsmen, would have enjoyed considerably greater property than the average member of his community. We can safely say that he would have owned his own house and farm, which provided a comfortable subsistence and probably a small surplus. He might have been a member of the church and was certainly active in town affairs, at least as a voter at town meetings if not as a holder of elective office. While his daily concerns centered on the affairs of his family and community, he was aware of the developing crisis between the American colonies and Great Britain. Because of the community consensus that was forming in the absence of little or no discussion of the alternatives, there was no question which side he would support when the break in relations actually came—as likely as not, if physically able, as a soldier. This is the sort of young man who experienced most immediately the meetinghouse tragedy.

The Ballad

❧ ❧

> But let us Some improvment make
> And to our Selves apply
> This awfull providence of god
> That Comes to us so nigh

*L*ess than three months before the meetinghouse tragedy, there appeared on the streets of Salem, Massachusetts, a printed broadside that would have provided ideal grist for Benjamin Franklin's satirical mill fifty years earlier or Mark Twain's a hundred years later. The broadside's fifteen wretched verses lament an episode of June 17 that, measured by loss of life, was even more tragic if perhaps less spectacular than Wilton's. Ten Salem people, including several married couples, had drowned while, as the author put it, "out on a Party of Pleasure." It is not hard to imagine what the young Silence Dogood or the creator of Huck Finn's friend Emmeline Grangerford and her "Ode to Stephen Dowling Bots" might have made of these samples of the Salem versifier's art:

> Yes, ten poor souls I've heard them say
>   Went lately to the Bottom.
> SALEM, O let it not be said
>   Their names were e'er Forgotton.

> May we not say Fifteen poor souls
>   Were plunged in the Sea,
> As Five th'unhappy women were
>   Advanced in Pregnancy.[1]

Compared to the "Friend to the Deceased" who composed the "Funeral Elegy," the rural poet who commemorated the Wilton meetinghouse tragedy was an able, even somewhat sophisticated writer. Few of his forty-three verses, though most are simple and unpolished, descend unintentionally into the burlesque. More to the point, the Wilton elegy constitutes, as the brief Salem one does not, a solid contribution to the Anglo-American ballad genre, one that the author obviously understood well.

The most significant difference between these two comparable efforts to commemorate a local tragedy, however, lies in the medium by which each was preserved and communicated. For the past five years, there had been a printing office in Salem, run by Samuel and Ebenezer Hall.[2] It was a simple matter for the Salem author to take his doggerel to the Halls' shop and have it quickly printed for sale on the streets. Because it was immediately set in type, it became permanently embalmed in a form that was identical in all its copies—especially since, for understandable reasons, there do not appear to have been any subsequent editions. By contrast, there was not a printing press within fifty miles of Wilton, nor was there a nearby bookseller or even a local post office. As far as anyone knows, the ballad did not see print for forty-five years, and then only in an obscure and incomplete fashion that certainly did not interrupt the life of the ballad that was still being perpetuated and subtly changed by more traditional and flexible means.

One such means, of course, was word of mouth. The featured speaker at Wilton's centennial celebration in 1839 asserted that the "somewhat antique melodies" of the ballad, "long after the event and within the memory of many now living . . . were familiarly sung by the young ladies of the town, as they carded and spun by their firesides."[3] Since only sixty-six years separated the accident from the centennial address, we may wonder actually how "long after the event" it was necessary for the verses to be sung in order to be recollected by persons living in 1839, but their persistence in the oral culture of the neighborhood was confirmed thirteen years later by the historian of New Ipswich, who wrote in 1852 that the "mournful ballad . . . was familiarly known and sung for many years afterwards." The point remains that the ballad lived at least for a while in the oral culture of Wilton and its neighboring communities. One wishes only that someone had noted the tune.[4]

There was yet another means of preservation and transmission, in what is now being called the "scribal culture." Clearly the first copy of the ballad was written down in the hand of its composer, whether it was Nathaniel Allen, Asa Black, an unnamed Massachusetts schoolteacher, or someone else.[5] It was copied with some frequency, by various persons and in one case possibly as a school penmanship exercise, from that time on.[6] The two extant manuscript copies known to me are not identical in every respect, nor are any of the various printed versions that must have been set from different manuscript copies at various times between 1818 and 1888.

The ballad, therefore, while apparently composed by a single author, underwent, during its transmission across generations by voice and by pen, various small alterations that would not have occurred had it been committed at once to print. In a very limited sense, it might be considered a species of local folklore. However, according to one authority, a "folksong" is understood as traditional material, meaning that it "must be in the possession of those in whose minds such material is stored—dependent for continuing existence on oral transmission."[7] The meetinghouse ballad, with its single authorship, its relatively short life compared to most true folksongs, and its scribal as well as oral transmission, is a "folksong" only by considerable stretching of the definition. Tristram P. Coffin, another folklore specialist, has noted that only a tiny proportion of ballads and local songs springing from a native tragedy or event survive long enough to be collected from tradition and mature into true folksongs with lives of their own. The survival of such a song in tradition depends upon its loss of uniqueness, since in a true folksong the importance of the event it commemorates becomes "less important than what should have happened. Even what an individual claims to have happened is less important than what the group or groups feel must have happened. Events are personal, subjective, unique; folk records of them are general, formulaic, trite." Thus for a local ballad to pass into folk tradition demands its transition into a story that is subject to infinite variations and applications with universal appeal.[8] Though the meetinghouse ballad does offer a universal lesson or two, its main importance is in its original purpose, the narration of a particular local event, the details of which do not change

standard pamphlet of sixteen small pages (a page on each side of each leaf) in one case and eight larger pages in the other. To the octavo signature is added a paper binding, hand decorated with a diamond design. Unlike the quarto version, which simply begins the untitled verses at the top of the first page, the octavo pamphlet contains, inside the cover, a title page, with the name of this copyist's presumed author, Asa Black, and decorated, again in conventional style for the period, with five black coffins representing the five whose deaths are commemorated. The octavo version does depart in one respect from printed pamphlet format. Because there is not room enough on the page to write each line across its width by hand, this scribe turned his pamphlet horizontally and wrote across what would normally be the length of the page instead; the reader, therefore, rather than turning pages right to left with the binding on his left, holds the pamphlet with the binding at the top. The quarto version, on the other hand, is written with the lines across the width of the page, so that the reader proceeds through the pamphlet in conventional fashion.

Clearly, therefore, both copyists intended their pamphlets, produced in the codex format that actually antedated Gutenberg but that by their time must have been associated almost inseparably in most minds with the practices of the print shop and bookbindery, to be permanent possessions, perhaps designed for multiple readerships.[12] Both of these copies also bear other marks of intended permanence and pride of possession. Each, for example, bears the name of the copyist. The octavo edition, which prominently displays the name of the presumed author on the title page, contains at the bottom of the first inside page, in smaller script after the end of the third stanza, a notation reading: "When this you see remember Solomon Lowell his scrabling." The "scrabler" made a somewhat similar entry on the next page, and his much larger and bolder signature appears at the end of the text. The quarto edition, the text of which is apparently done in ink over a trial run in pencil, is inscribed in a large space at the bottom of the second page, "Polly Lewis her verses," with the date of May 24, 1779. Contrary to the presumptions of our own time, the possessive pronoun seems to have connoted not authorship, but merely ownership of this particular copy. Polly herself may not

FIGURE 16. *Title page of the Asa Black copy of the meetinghouse ballad, owned formerly by Clarke Blair and now by the University of New Hampshire. The date in the title, September 17, is erroneous. Photo by Clarke Blair.*

even have been the copyist, since her signature and declaration of ownership is in a different hand than that of the text. The last page documents a transfer of ownership: "Phebe Howard her verses given to her July ye 25, 1779." One can only conclude that Polly Lewis made a gift of the copy to Phebe two months after the copy had come into her possession. Moreover, it appears that Polly, whoever she was, may actually have intended her copy to be a gift for Phebe on the occasion of her birth, since she was born only the previous March 17. Phebe's inscription was obviously added years later, as was the couplet that not only identifies the manuscript pamphlet as a "book" but also proclaims her very self-conscious possession of it: "Phebe Howard her Book and Name / All you that look may see the same."

The history of the ballad's publishing in print, such as it is, is quickly told. It begins, apparently, in 1818. Nathaniel Coverly, Jr., the surviving member of a long father-son partnership of printers and publishers, brought out a news broadside describing the burning of the Exchange Coffee House, "the pride and ornament of Boston." The broadside—entitled "Tremendous fire!!"—was illustrated with a dramatic woodcut showing the seven-story building in flames. On the reverse side was printed "Wilton Tragedy," consisting of thirty-one of the ballad's forty-three stanzas.[13] Chances are that Coverly's acquaintance with the ballad had come during the brief period that he and his father were in business in Amherst, New Hampshire, in 1795 and 1796, when they began the first newspaper in that part of the state, *The Amherst Journal and New Hampshire Advertiser*.[14]

The ballad then appeared successively, in whole or in part, at the end of the printed version of the Rev. Ephraim Peabody's Wilton Centennial Address (1839), in a New Ipswich town history (1852), in the *New England Historical and Genealogical Register* (1868), in a genealogy of the Fletcher family (1881), in Wilton's town history (1888), and in *Yankee* magazine (1970).[15]

Only two of these printed versions, those in *NEHGR* and in the Wilton history, are close to complete. Each contains forty-two stanzas, one fewer than the number in both manuscript versions. There are minor differences between these two printed versions, an indication that each was copied from a different source. The contributor to *NEHGR* claimed that his was the complete ballad, copied from the same manuscript that provided the ten stanzas at the end of Peabody's centennial address. Variations in wording, however, together with Peabody's almost apologetic explanation that he was recording only "such stanzas as can be recovered from the poem," make that assertion very questionable indeed. The version in the Wilton history was purportedly copied from a manuscript found in Topsham, Vermont. We are left with the strong probability that each of the seven printed versions, all of which ex-

tember ye 17, 1773." The other manuscript copy, while bound up in booklet fashion like the first, carries no title at all. The 1818 broadside is entitled "Wilton Tragedy." A version apparently copied from yet another manuscript copy in an 1888 history of Wilton was originally entitled "on the unhappy accident which happened at the raising of Wilton meeting-house," though it is not clear that that was all there was to it. Another partial version in the New Ipswich town history of 1852 is untitled. Since these verses do not specifically mourn or even recollect any of the deceased by name or as a group as much as they report and reflect upon the event itself (but the same is true of the Salem verses, which bear the same title), "elegy" may not be the best term our eighteenth-century author or copyist could have come up with. However, in the more general sense of responding dolefully to death, portions of it do incorporate the elegiac tradition, and since the copy carrying that title appears to have been copied from another, apparently that was the one used during part of the ballad's life in the scribal culture, though certainly not all of it.[21]

The ballad is structured with great care. It opens with a formulaic invitation to the reader—or rather, the listener: "Attention give and you shall *hear* / A melancholy theme." This is one form of a standard ballad opening, one that announces that what follows is worth listening to. It is a variation on the more familiar "Come all ye [jolly seamen, noble warriors, pretty maidens, roving bachelors, or whatever category of listener was appropriate]" or "Come listen to my story . . . ," not essential to the ballad format, but frequently used nevertheless.[22] The second couplet of the first stanza, "Tis such an instance as there is / But very seldom seen," assures the hearer that the story he is about to be told is interesting because the event, besides being "melancholy," is rare. Moreover, the listener at this point is invited by the word "seen" not only to hear about the event but to be present, as it were, as a spectator. The implication is strong that the author, speaking through the singer, is claiming authority by virtue of having been an actual eyewitness. The second stanza is another introductory one, taking the first two lines ("In seventeen Hundred seventy-three / September seventh Day") to establish the date much in the manner of the early twentieth-century poet who thus opened his commemoration of the disastrous munitions ship explosion that devastated Halifax in 1917: "It was on the sixth of December, nineteen hundred and seventeen / That Halifax suffered disaster, the worst she'd ever seen."[23] The second half of the Wilton stanza not only announces the place but also signals that a lesson in theology is coming along with the story: "At Wilton did Almity God / His anger there Display."

The third and fourth stanzas plunge into the narrative. A "Great Collection" of men has met to raise a meetinghouse (whose religious but not civic function is detailed), nearly completing, with divine help, the raising of the frame: "And joyfull they became." Whether there is a subtle hint here that it was a rum-inspired joy is impossible to say, but even if that was the author's meaning of "joyful," it was almost certainly not meant in these pre-temperance years to be judgmental. The fifth stanza repeats the elation of the raising crew at this nearly completed stage of its task, but its foreboding third and fourth lines serve as a grim transition: "poor souls they did but little think / They were so nigh their graves."

The sixth stanza begins the long middle section of the ballad, detailing the accident and the injuries interspersed with occasional allusions both to mourning and to eternal rewards and punishments. "All on a Sudden a beam broak," begins the jarring stanza. By 1852, someone had improved the meter of one version to "All on a sudden broke a beam,"[24] but that variation appears in no other version known to me. Then follow twenty-one stanzas evoking the horror of the event, alluding to the fifty-three victims, the gruesome injuries, the five deaths in their proper sequence (but without names), the mourning of the survivors, and hopeful but measured speculation about the eternal fate of the deceased. The author, in fact, established a pattern for the use of this last pious embellishment in each of the stanzas, the twelfth through the fourteenth, that reported one or more deaths:

> One in an instantly was kild
> His soul has taken flight
> To Mantions of Eternal day
> Or everlasting night

> Two more in a few moments Spent
> Did bid this world adieu
> wich are rejected of their god
> Or with his Chosen few

> two more in a Short time did pass
> threw death's dark shady vail
> which now are in the realmns of joy
> or the infernal Hell

These three "death" stanzas are followed immediately by three more expressing hope that in each case it is the first of the eternal alternatives that has prevailed, using a clever play on the word "fall," which in its second appearance is susceptible to two meanings:

> but we must hope their precious Souls
> are with their Saviour dear
> reeping the fruites, the blessed frutes
> Of faithfull Servants here

> And if this be their happy Case
> Glory to God be given
> O blessed day, o happy fall
> That Sent there Souls to heaven

> Where there's no danger of a fall
> And nothing to molest
> No care no grief for to desturb
> Their ever lasting rest

By contrast, the victims' survivors are left to mourn, and so stanza eighteen links the passages on death and eternity with those detailing the various categories of earthly mourners:

> While their dear friends are bowed down
> With Sorrow for there Sake
> Grieving and mourning til there hearts
> are ready for to brake

The categories are five, to which is added a sixth in the 1818 printed version; each is accorded a four-line stanza: widows, children, fathers, mothers, brothers and sisters, and, in 1818, "one maiden lover." Then comes another transitional stanza summoning compassion for the bereaved, indeed asserting that the readers' "hearts will melt if they are not / as hard as any Stone." (Here the verb "read" instead of "hear" is used.) But sympathy of this sort cannot be removed for long from reflection on the fate of the dead victims. And so from meditating upon earthly suffering, the reader is commanded to turn his attention once more to the "Eternal unseen world":

Remember well the mournfull scean
   And melancholy day
In which the almighty Sent grim death
   and took there Souls away

To the Eternal unseen world
   To spend eternity
Of un expressed fellisety
   or boundless misery

according as their works have bin
   in this vinyard of the Lord
So they receive of God there Judg
   there right and just reward.

Our amateur poet-theologian is apparently unbothered by the technical contradiction between the distinctly Arminian message of these last lines and the more orthodox notion in stanza thirteen that the dead are "rejected of their God / Or with his chosen few." But more of that later. We need now to move to the conclusion of the ballad, which like a good Puritan sermon consists of a separate section headed "improvement" in one manuscript version and "application" in the other. It constitutes about a third of the ballad, fourteen or fifteen stanzas, depending on whether one of them has been inserted, as it was in some versions, earlier in the poem.

Here is a lengthy contribution to the ubiquitous theme of *memento mori*, most familiar to the casual modern observer in early gravestone art or perhaps in Jonathan Edwards' chilling application of Deuteronomy 32:35, "Their foot shall slide in due time."[25] This was not an element of the much shorter Funeral Elegy commemorating the Salem drownings earlier in the year, but that author obviously felt his duty unfulfilled until he had added a prose explanation of the event, concluding with a plea for "making a right improvement of such an awful warning as this from GOD, who is continually saying not only by this but by many other awakening dispensations and calls, Be ye also ready." In the last third of the meetinghouse ballad, as at the end of one of the newspaper accounts of the event, the Wilton tragedy is transformed from a terrible drama and cause for lamentation to an awakening dispensation.

The opening stanza, which appears as the epigraph of this

chapter (the first word is "Come" in some versions rather than "But"), announces the purpose of what follows ("improvement"), and the next several stanzas proclaim in a variety of ways that death is inescapable, and may well come, as for the five victims, suddenly. At that point, we shall " . . . meet omnipotence / To have our doom pronounced and to/Receive our recompense." Therefore, we should all be prepared.

At this point the author enlarges upon the doctrine to which he has alluded just before the improvement section begins, essentially a theology of works:

> And if our deeds have evil been
> We Shall receive this doom
> depart from me I know you not
> for you did me disown
>
> Down Down into a deep abiss
> of wo and misery
> Our Souls are plung'd there to remain
> throughout eternity
>
> An Angry god is pouring forth
> the vials of his wrath
> and indignation upon us
> Which is the Second death
>
> Therefore as we must all be judg'd
> According as we have done
> tis highly needfull for us all
> The Christian race to run

The right preparation, therefore, consists of good works, but the author is sufficiently orthodox to insist that such works be the product, if not of conversion, at least of commitment to the faith of the New Testament. "Put on brest plates of righteousness," he writes, paraphrasing Paul's epistle to the Ephesians, "And take the shield of faith, / The spirit's sword for to defend / us in the narrow path." This spiritual emphasis continues in the following stanza:

> Let us be making peace with god
> while we have life and breath
> that so we may prepaired be
> To meet a Sudden death

Two stanzas next portray the bliss of heaven, contrasting conventionally with the earlier depiction of the unbearable miseries of hell. With images of "joy and bliss," "clear Streams," and "heavenly Love" fresh in mind, the reader is conveyed to the final stanza:

> That this be our happy Case
> When we this life do end
> God grant of his Infinite grace
> threw Jesus Christ Amen

Here the modern reader's eye is drawn first to the surprising, almost comical use of the formulaic prayer ending that constitutes the last line. But what of the line that precedes it, the one that speaks of God's infinite grace (which in order to scan properly would have to be spoken, or sung, "in-FI-nite grace," probably with a long *i*)? Is the writer an orthodox Calvinist after all? Does this assertion of salvation by grace, which seems to square better with the "chosen few" of the thirteenth stanza than with the more numerous passages that appear to portray heaven as reward, mean that the author is trying to have it both ways in order to appeal to readers of either persuasion? Or is he trying imperfectly to convey the nuances of the difficult old New England doctrine that faith-based works are a sign, but not the cause, of election? Or is he, as many laymen and not a few clergymen in this liberalizing era undoubtedly were, just theologically confused?

Or, to add to this list of questions a purely rhetorical one, is this really the point? Do these questions have a useful answer? Rather than trying to analyze the author's intellectual position (and shortcomings) within the framework of formal theology, perhaps we should turn our attention to what the ballad, as an expression of the popular culture of the time and place, can tell us about that culture. First, as we have already noted at some length, it was a culture that recognized and took for granted its participation in the Anglo-American ballad tradition. Judging by similar efforts elsewhere in the region, the composition of a serious ballad was an entirely natural response to a dramatic event such as the meetinghouse tragedy. It should be noted that this response was not that of one of the community's learned or "literary" men, such as a clergyman, but that of a literate but unpolished writer, probably one without poetic pretensions. He was simply participating, in an entirely natural way and with unusual success, in a fairly common activity.

It was also a culture that recognized and appreciated pathos. The fact of death is not so much the point as the horror of its circumstance, and most especially the mournful plight of the bereaved relatives. There is no attempt to avoid sentimentality; the reader is in fact encouraged repeatedly to shed a sympathetic tear with those who have suffered loss.

And it was a culture that feared God, more in his character as Judge than as Father. There is more than a hint of old-time New England providentialism in the opening stanza ("At Wilton did Almity God / His anger there Display"). The fact that the theme is not sustained, probably attributable at least in part to the literary shortcomings of the author, does not lessen its impact. The idea that divine judgment was at work in the accident requires no embellishment; it is taken for granted. But if God the Father (the "Almity") is an angry judge, Jesus is the compassionate savior. It is he to whom the prayer for temporal mercy is addressed in the tenth stanza, it is he with whom the more fortunate victims are imagined to be in Heaven, and it is he through whom, in the prayer with which the ballad ends, it is hoped God's grace will be administered. This is no scholastic rendering of the Trinity, especially since the Third Person is absent, nor even of the relationship between Father and Son, who seem to be understood as quite separate and unequal. It is merely a common-sense and somewhat coarse rendition of these two aspects of the divine nature, cast in terms that do not stretch a layman's understanding, that the poet and his forebears had undoubtedly heard in more nuanced terms for many generations.

Likewise the ballad's treatment of salvation. For the balladist to fret over the distinction between grace and works would be entirely out of character. He used the language of both, especially when it suited the purposes of rhyme or meter, because he had heard both from the pulpit, no doubt with a changing emphasis to which neither he nor his neighbors had given much thought, over the course of his lifetime. If the formal theology of his time was veering toward Arminianism, to culminate eventually in Arianism, this was not a concern of the ballad. Nor was it probably even understood by most members of that community. As of 1773, it will be remembered, the Wilton church covenant, accepted by a congregation that comprised a third of the town's entire population, was unspecific on such matters.[26] If anything, the ballad's vestigial use of occasional Calvinist phrases ("chosen few," "infinite grace") was at variance with the town's official teaching, but in this very practical community the recognition of that tension would have required an uncharacteristic exercise in theological nit-picking. It was enough that the ballad express a conventional but sincere piety, that it bow to the will of God, and that it affirm a life after death with a system of divine rewards and punishments.

The ballad, therefore, neither learned nor "folk," is the best expression we have of a vernacular response to the meetinghouse tragedy.

After the Fall

❦ ❧

Remember well the mournfull Scean
and melancholy day
In which the almighty sent grim death
and took there Souls away

Wilton did remember the mournful scene for quite some time, and so did its neighboring communities. The ballad, we recall, was transmitted by pen and by word of mouth, and remembrance of the event ritualized by singing it at least for two or three generations. The slave Caesar heard a scream that "rung in his ears for years after." Like his black New Ipswich neighbor Boston, who dramatically and emotionally narrated Bible stories whenever there was reason for a public gathering, Caesar on such occasions, "with great feeling, almost of horror," told the story of the meetinghouse.[1] The memory of the tragedy was sufficiently alive, though probably fading, to be included in Abiel Livermore's dedication sermon for a replacement meetinghouse (comparable buildings were usually called "churches" by then) in 1861, and in his and Sewall Putnam's *History of Wilton* in 1888.

What the record does not provide, perhaps because the experience of war and wartime casualties soon overshadowed the significance of the meetinghouse tragedy in the life the community, are materials enabling us to gauge the communal economic and social, or even emotional impact of the sudden loss of life and limb on such a scale. The subsequent history of the meetinghouse project, however, suggests both a tough-minded stoicism and a quick recovery from what at first must have seemed a terrible physical blow to the most able-bodied members of the population. It also suggests the overriding importance, tempered by Yankee frugality and practicality, that the community placed upon having an adequate house of worship and public meeting.

While in the immediate aftermath of the accident the raising was "put by for the present," to use the words of the *Massachusetts Spy*,[2] the postponement did not last long. In accordance with New England custom, the town responded to the event with a day of fasting and prayer, perhaps as early as two days after the accident, more likely on Thursday, September 16.[3] Not many days later, a somewhat altered building crew was assembled to continue the raising.

First, a new beam had to be found to replace the broken one. The right tree having been properly hewn and mortised, the crew began the hard work of raising the forty-five-foot timber by block and tackle to the plate, twenty-seven feet above the ground Once again, there was ample reason to doubt whether the new meetinghouse was ever meant to be—and new fuel for the superstitious. Scarcely had the beam reached the level of the plate when some piece of the lifting apparatus gave way. Again, unbelievably, the huge beam intended for the central overhead position hurtled to the ground. Nobody was either on it or under it, so this time there were no injuries. Nor, apparently, was the beam itself damaged beyond use. This second accident, however, did give the workmen and the community pause. "They soon, however, recovered from this state of excessive trepidation," wrote Wilton's minister and historian in 1822, "and proceeded to business, until the frame was completed without any other accident."[4]

The next step was to sheath the frame, allowing for the building's forty-five windows and three doors, with broad inch-thick boards, probably sawed from pine or hemlock logs at Jacob Putnam's sawmill, located on a stream not more than a mile by road north of the common.[5] The boards for the walls were nailed horizontally across the frame, the roof boards also horizontally along the length of the building, bearing on both principal and common rafters. After the sheathing came shingles for the roof and clapboards for the sides of the building, possibly including the closed-in two-story stair "porch" at the east end.[6] As had the sawn boards, shingles and clapboards had been provided by the winning bidders—by "vendue," to use the contemporary term—and paid for out of the 150 pounds, with subsequent supplements, that the town meeting had appropriated for building materials back in 1772. Both had been riven with froe and wooden mallet from short lengths of straight-grained logs, probably the more readily available white pine rather than the more durable cedar, and then smoothed by plane or drawknife. Normal practice would have called for each length of clapboard, rather short by comparison with the sawn clapboards of our own day, also to have been thinned by shaving (or "skived") at each end in order to make a waterproof joint by overlapping the similarly treated ends of its neighbors.[7] Naturally, boards, clapboards, shingles, and the necessary nails had been provided and brought to the site beforehand, as were the doors and glazed windows, and perhaps the prefashioned pedimented main doorframe as well, but considering the size of the building and the time-consuming nature of all the manual tasks associated with its finishing, it was not a job that could be done quickly.

Then there was the problem of money, which was running short, and questions about spending and accounting. As early as October 23, a town meeting was asked to decide "what further sum of money" would be appropriated to finish the meetinghouse. The voters refused to appropriate any, but did approve the selectmen's proposal to apply some outstanding taxes to the project when collected. On January 18, the selectmen, still worried about finishing the outside of the building and apparently beginning to doubt the building committee's stewardship of funds, asked another special meeting not only to appoint a committee to examine the building accounts but also to dismiss the current building committee and replace it with another one. The voters approved both proposals. At the end of what must have been an especially contentious meeting, just before adjourning to a further session three weeks thence, the voters decided to reinstate the original building committee after all, only to reverse themselves once more at the February session. To meet the mounting expenses of the meetinghouse project, the town approved the selectmen's proposal to borrow the town's "school money."[8]

At the same time, a full two months before any decisions had been made about finishing and furnishing the inside of the building, the voters took up the sale of pews. As in all such projects of the time, the provision and sale of family pews, those box-shaped enclosures with doors and with benches all round the inside, would be the main source of funds. Though it would be many months before the pews would be built, it was now time to decide how they would be assigned and, more important, begin the process that would bring in the necessary revenue, especially since the town had just voted to put itself in debt to its own school account.

When a man bought a pew, he was buying not just the wooden structure in which his family sat, but the "ground" beneath it. Just as if he were buying a cemetery lot, a place to build a house, or an entire farm, he was buying a piece of real estate, conveyed to him by deed from the town to be transmitted by will to his heirs. In Wilton, purchasers of pew "ground" were given the option of making their own provisions for building materials, though not free reign to design and embellish as one wished. Despite the undeniable hierarchy of wealth and importance within this community of neighbors, its egregious display in the meetinghouse was unacceptable.

Hierarchy, however, could be and was expressed in a subtle way, in the location of one's pew. Even in the assignment of pews, however, distinctions were vague, flexible, and, within the limits of one's ability and willingness to pay, dependent upon personal choice. In the more developed towns of New England, "seating" in earlier times had been by assignment, the more favorably located, often larger pews going to families of the greatest acknowledged dignity and so on down the line. The people of Wilton, however, like those in other more recently settled towns in this part of the region, had long since outgrown, if they recalled at all, the rigid system of social class that had once governed seating. Now it was the principles of the open market. Except for the minister, whose family was deferentially accorded the pew at the foot of the pulpit stairs, the townsmen submitted bids on the right to choose a pew. The highest bidder or bidders, according to a vote of January 18, 1774, took "their Choice throughout the whole." Though Wilton was in some respects a democratic (though not egalitarian) society, it was still very much a closed one. "None but inhabitants who are freeholders," the town voted, "should be allowed to bid on or purchase any pew."[9]

By April, the outside of the meetinghouse, now being supervised by a new building committee, was far enough along that attention could be devoted to the inside of the building. The new committee consisted of the brothers William and Jacob Abbot, the first a sitting selectman and his brother a former selectman, and Jonathan Burton, a frequent town officeholder. The voters now appointed the same committee to finish the inside and directed that the walls should be "ceiled"—that is, wainscoted—from the floor to the bottom of the windows both on the main level and in the galleries.[10] Presumably the upper part of the walls and the ceiling were to be "plaistered," to use the warrant's term, though no action on that point is recorded.

This is the first mention in the record of galleries, but there can be no question that the installation of upper-level seating in what today might more likely be called a "balcony" was understood from the beginning. Without the intent to build galleries, there would have been no need for the building's twenty-seven-foot height or second tier of windows, and the debates over "porches," whose main function was to provide stairways to the galleries, would have been meaningless. In short, the Wilton meetinghouse was planned, inside and out, much in accordance with standard New England meetinghouse design at the time. The galleries, projecting from the upper wall around three sides of the interior—the broad side opposite the pulpit and along each of the narrow ends—were supported by posts, or columns, resting on the meetinghouse floor.

Those columns posed a problem for at least two of the pew purchasers, both of whom turned to the town for compensation. When Thomas Russell and the young selectman William Abbot discovered in January 1775 that some of the space in the pews they had bought would be occupied by two of the posts that supported the gallery, they petitioned the town for abatements "in consideration of the pillars standing in the same." The townsmen voted instead to take the two pews back, presumably to be sold to less particular buyers.[11]

In some meetinghouses, the galleries contained at least some family box pews like those on the main level,[12] but the Wilton voters rejected that idea and voted instead to build "long pews" (like modern church pews) in the galleries and sell rights to occupy them. Gallery seating, unlike that in the family pews on the main floor, was divided by gender, men on one side, women on the other. Thus Daniel Kenney paid twelve shillings, eleven pence for "one Right on the Mens side in the front," meaning that even the gallery across the broad front side was divided in the middle between men's and women's sections, while John Cram, bidding on rights to the "side" galleries, those on the narrow ends that faced each other across the meetinghouse, paid one pound, six shillings, eight pence for "three Rights Two on the Mens side and One on the Womens Side." They were among the thirty-five people, including one woman, Abigail Burton, who bought from one to seven "rights" in the gallery pews at an auction on January 3, 1775. The seven were bought by Francis Putnam, who bought seven "front" pew rights, three on the men's side and four on the women's side, all for four pounds, eleven shillings.[13]

The one other great furnishing, the details of which the remaining record too dimly illuminates, was the raised pulpit, reached by a short flight of stairs from the meetinghouse floor, backed by a centered window at pulpit (rather than floor or gallery) level, and embellished for acoustical purposes by a sounding board suspended overhead.[14] The pulpit, the most conspicuous feature of the interior—for in Puritan worship it was the word of God as interpreted by the pastor and teacher of the community that always held center stage—was fixed in the center of the broad north wall opposite the front door.[15] We can be certain that this most important appurtenance, like everything else about the meetinghouse, was carefully structured from the best available "stuff," for what New Englanders rejected by way of ecclesiastical art and embellishments they compensated for in solidity, craftsmanship, and quiet dignity. Though not often articulated, this essentially religious value in meetinghouse construction occasionally found voice. As early as 1742 the inhabitants of what would eventually become Keene, New Hampshire, having agreed four years earlier to finish their new meetinghouse and its furnishings "completely workman-like," now voted to substitute paneled doors for the plain ones originally planned, and to provide the main entrance with a double door instead of a single one. The building committee was instructed to "agree with a man to do it well, and decently, as becomes such a house."[16]

Once all these preparations had been made, it was time to appoint what would today be called a sexton to have custody of the keys, sweep the building, and "take care of the Christian-ing Bason." It was also time to dispose of the old log meetinghouse, now about to be abandoned, and to see about adding still further to the dignity of this now revamped civic space by putting up a notice board, or, in the words of the selectmen, "a Post in some place near the meetinghouse in order to stick papers on and likewise a Handsome South [sun]dial." From now on, this would be the constable's official posting place for town warrants.[17]

On January 5, 1775, a Thursday, a year and four months after the frame collapsed, the day at last arrived when the community would take its seats in the handsome new structure to hear the Reverend Mr. Livermore's dedication sermon. The sermon, together with Mr. Livermore's unrecorded fast day address shortly after the accident and certain features of the "Letter from New Ipswich" that comprised the earliest published news report of the event, add another dimension to the community's response to the meetinghouse tragedy.

There was, in the first place, a response governed by folklore. Reaching far back into an uncodified body of assumptions and beliefs from both his European and his African heritage, the "mulatto man" whose bowl had broken under his dancing feet interpreted that small event as a dreadful omen. We can be sure that when the dancer's prediction of calamity was almost instantly fulfilled, "Old Caesar" was not alone among the spectators who reacted in superstitious terror. Then there was the "cursed tree" that had killed Isaac Russell and apparently now was responsible for the accident that killed five more and injured forty-eight. And there was the falling of the second beam as it was being raised to replace the one that had broken. However much the clergy of several generations may have decried any assumption of preternatural forces at work in either of these events, such assumptions were obviously present in the community. Inspired by some distorted remnant of the providential theology of an earlier day in New England or by deep-seated folk assumptions of a much earlier time than that, quite a few discerned in the tragedy either the hand of a perturbed deity or the influence of evil forces.

I have argued that the ballad at the center of this account of the meetinghouse tragedy was not a "folksong" in the usual sense because it was composed by a definite author, because it survived only in a very limited and localized sense in what could accurately be called "folk" memory, and because its interest and importance depend entirely upon the single historical event it describes. It never, in other words, transcended that particular event; it was never, like a true folk ballad, universalized by adaptation.[18] However, the author did draw upon a folk medium, the narrative ballad, and used (rather well) the most common traditional ballad meter in which to tell his story. To that extent, we may say that the most conspicuous and interesting response to the tragedy, while not a species of folklore itself, drew in genre and form upon deeply rooted folk traditions.

I have urged that the message of the ballad be considered an expression of another dimension of culture—a second level, if you prefer—namely, the "popular" or the "vernacular." Either term will do, since in this case they both apply, though their meanings are not identical. The first, in the sense intended here, refers to an expression grounded in the lives and thoughts of the common people, the ordinary folk comprising the vast majority, who, in this instance, shared a communal consciousness and did the practical work of the community whether in or out of the home. The second emphasizes the local rather than the common; a "vernacular" expression is one that is indigenous to a particular place or people. Both terms suggest a dimension of culture that is distinct both from that rooted entirely in folk memory, though either could comprehend folklore as well as other expressions, and from that which is the formal and learned. Like the meetinghouse itself, designed by a committee of ordinary townsmen in conformity with a distinct but still evolving regional style and constructed by an army of practical workmen who drew upon skills and methods many of them had developed on their own farms, the ballad reflected at once the "popular" and the "vernacular."

While lacking a formal or even a consistent theology, the ballad is concerned mainly with drawing religious lessons from the meetinghouse tragedy. Those lessons, which we may take as reflections of popular understandings of the time and place, are several: the agency of God, explicitly described as "angry," in human calamity; the salvific role of Jesus in both temporal and eternal realms; some recognition of the doctrine of election; a much greater emphasis upon the doctrine of rewards and punishments, stating more or less explicitly that one who has lived a virtuous life will be rewarded with heaven and one who has lived otherwise will be punished in hell; a connection, not drawn very clearly, between the achievement of virtue and the practice of Christianity; the need to recognize the imminence of death and thus to be spiritually prepared. None of these ideas would have been seriously at odds with what various New England clerics would have preached at one time or another over the past century and a half. It is doubtful, however, that one would have heard all of them being preached from the same pulpit at the same time; as we have noticed, the ballad lacks theological consistency. It also lacks, for the most part, those scriptural garnishings with which ministers demonstrated not only their own learning but, more important, the authority and support for their pronouncements. Even the first published news account of the accident, which we have speculated was written by the minister of New Ipswich, discloses a biblical sophistication, with its clever juxtaposition of a pair of Old and New Testament quotations at the end, which is noticeably absent from the ballad.

In addition to the responses grounded in folklore and those expressing the popular culture of the time and place, there was a learned, formal response—the closest a rural New England community of the eighteenth century would come to what might be called "high" culture. Unhappily, the text of Mr. Livermore's fast day sermon, written in the immediate aftermath of the accident, does not survive. We do, however, know his text, the opening line of Psalm 127: "Except the Lord build the house, they labor in vain that build it." [19] We cannot know what specific lesson the minister drew from the Psalm on that occasion. Obviously, it gave ample opportunity to suggest that the Lord had improperly been left out of the project. The choice of text, however, while it seems to emphasize the necessity of divine help and favor in an enterprise, does not necessarily imply the possibility of divine revenge. The popular ballad, of course, did draw such a lesson from the event; so would have the minister's Puritan predecessors before Harvard had become liberal. Whatever Mr. Livermore's message may have been that day, however (one hopes that it contained at least a measure of consolation for the bereaved), we can guess that it was somewhat different in emphasis from, but not inconsistent with, the outright optimism of his dedication sermon in 1775, in which he inserted at one point the same quotation from the Psalms.

The theme of the dedication sermon reflected well the text upon which it was based, "For all things come of thee, and of thine own have we given thee." [20] Its message was neither repentance for some imagined offense nor an acknowledgment of divine retribution, but simple gratitude to God. Providence had smiled upon the undertaking of the meetinghouse, now to be dedicated, even "sanctified," for holy use. [21]

Leaving aside for the moment Mr. Livermore's rather more sanguine vision of the deity than that of either the folk or the popular theologies discussed here, we might pause to notice the distance he had come from earlier New England concepts of the meetinghouse itself. To a seventeenth-century Puritan, no place was holier than any other. The meetinghouse was just that, a place for church and town to meet—latter-day New Englanders were still using the term in 1773 and would continue to do so for several decades to come—but not sacred space, or at least no more sacred than any other space. Yet Mr. Livermore spoke of assembling "to sanctify and set apart this house . . . to be acknowledged and improved as a house of prayer." He prayed that God would "fill this house with his glory," that he "own . . . [it] as his sanctuary," and that "he will from time to time meet with us herein and enable us to worship him in spirit and in truth." He made no mention of the secular uses to which the building would be put. This language of sanctification may have gone over the heads of the congregation or been dismissed as insignificant, but it discloses to us one aspect of a subtle reorientation in Puritan thinking that would be completed, in this aspect, with the common adoption in the 1830s and 1840s of the term "church" among former dissenting groups to apply to their places of worship.[22] By the twentieth century, the Congregationalist successors to the Puritans had carried the concept a step further by referring to the room in which worship was carried on, as distinct from other spaces in the "church" building, as the "sanctuary."[23]

Let us return to Mr. Livermore's treatment of the role of God in the building of the meetinghouse, and in the meetinghouse tragedy in particular. After recounting in standard form, with ample biblical allusions, the many examples of Israel in the dedication of its tabernacles and temples, the preacher concluded that Christians have even greater cause to "rejoice when provision is made for the convenient carrying on and performing that true spiritual worship which Christ has set up in the room of the Jewish ritual." Surely, he went on, paraphrasing several passages from the letters of Paul, "they that have the kingdom and interest of Christ at heart, and truly desire to see the Christian worship carried on with a becoming decency and order, have just ground, yea, the greatest reason, to rejoice and be glad to see comfortable provision made herefor."[24]

Since the meetinghouse was now completed, and since it was only "by the concurring smiles of . . . Providence that we obtain any good," the dedication is above all else an occasion for gratitude. Probably to the surprise of some of his hearers, Mr. Livermore was able to say that God had "remarkably smiled upon us while we have been building this house." Primarily, it turns out, the weather had cooperated: there was ample rain during the growing season when it was needed, but "remarkable dryness of the season in the latter part of the summer" to facilitate "the carrying on of the work." By this time, after Mr. Livermore had been preaching about forty-five minutes, many in the congregation must have been wondering whether their minister would ever mention the events of September 1773. That moment finally came. "It is true," he acknowledged in the midst of his praise of a

benevolent deity, "we met with a most grievous disaster in erecting the frame which we ought never to forget." But, he continued
with what was surely an acute awareness of how the tragedy had
been received in the popular religious consciousness, "whether
we ought to consider it as a rebuke of Providence is a matter of in-
quiry." Here at work was the mind of one who had been trained
in argumentation and the use of evidence, now urging his people
not to leap to unfounded conclusions. Of his own conclusion,
however, there was more than a hint:

So much mercy was displayed in the midst of the judgment that it evidently
appears that we suffered far less than we deserved for our careless and presumptuous neglect of the proper means of safety. View it in what light you
will, nine-tenths of the men who were in the midst of the danger must acknowledge that they experienced as much of the goodness and mercy of God,
in escaping with their lives, as ever they experienced; but still we must acknowledge the hand of God, both in inclining us to undertake this work, and
in succeeding and prospering us in carrying it on, for, "except the Lord build
the house, they labor in vain who build it."[25]

With the rationalism of most educated men of his era, Mr. Livermore places the cause of the accident not on divine judgment
but on costly human error. By this time, though there is little evidence elsewhere in the record to show it except perhaps the dismissal of the original building committee early in 1774, there must
have been a community consensus that there had been careless
mistakes and misjudgments at the raising. The minister was perhaps reflecting the common understanding of the community on
that point and urging his listeners to think of this human failing,
intellectual rather than moral, as the real cause of the accident. If
God did judge, it was the sort of judgment that works through the
operation of natural causes and effects, in this case altogether
preventable simply by the exercise of proper human reason and
skill. But Mr. Livermore wanted to talk less about divine judgment, at least in connection with the meetinghouse raising, than
about divine mercy. As a liberal, he was far more comfortable
dealing with this side of the equation. God had indeed been present at the raising, guarding the great majority of the workers from
death in the midst of destruction and chaos. There was no mention of the other forty-eight injuries.

Truly, in the preacher's hands, God was a benevolent being.

But saving the lives of a hundred or so workmen was only a sign of that fact, evidence for refuting the popular notion of divine vengeance. The substantive truth that "the Lord build[s] the house" lay in the divine gift of life and talent, the proper use of which is a human responsibility:

> Let us acknowledge that it is God who has made us, and furnished us with all our talents; that if we have properly improved them, this is owing to his gracious influence. That it is entirely owing to his influence and assistance that we have built this house. Therefore, we ourselves and the house which we have built are all his property.

It follows, of course, that the community is obliged to use God's house properly, thankfully, and devoutly, and "to offer proper Christian sacrifices here."[26]

Thus Wilton's most significant learned response to the tragedy was Arminian in temperament, perhaps tending even toward the Unitarianism that the town, under a new minister, would eventually adopt. It was biblically informed, rationally grounded, and theologically quite sophisticated. By comparison with its constant stress upon a beneficent and merciful God, its references to Christ seem muted, almost pro forma. We recall some of the stridently evangelical passages in the ballad, invoking Jesus in both an earthly and a heavenly salvific role as a counterpoint to the awful judgment of God, presumably God the Father. The sermon contains nothing of this sort (except for one reference to "Him who bought us with his own blood"), nor does it speak as the ballad does of an afterlife, though we can perhaps acknowledge that a meetinghouse dedication may not have been an appropriate occasion for the discussion of such a topic.

But while the minister virtually discounts the possibility that divine wrath was at work in the fall of the meetinghouse frame, he claims that it might be in the country's public affairs. This was 1775. The army occupying Boston had already seized a store of provincial arms in Charlestown, a Provincial Congress and Committee of Safety had been formed in Massachusetts, minutemen had been organized, and Paul Revere's first ride, this one to the north, had resulted in a raid by New Hampshire men upon the King's fort in Portsmouth Harbor just three weeks before the Wilton meetinghouse dedication. While Boston remained under military occupation, royal government in New Hampshire had already been rendered ineffective. Lexington and Concord were but three months in the future.

At the end of his sermon, in startling contrast to all that had come before, Mr. Livermore proclaimed that ". . . the judgments of God are now abroad in the earth, and his rod is upon our land. God is now threatening to deprive us of our liberty and privileges, or to reduce us to the dreadful extremity of engaging in a civil war . . . with our mother country, which is vastly more terrible than a war with a foreign adversary."[27]

The main reason for this patriotic outburst, with its intimation of divine wrath that had been lacking up till now, illuminates yet another side of New England's rural culture. Mr. Livermore's allusion to the impending Revolutionary crisis comes in the midst of a warning to the "young and gay," a sort of coda with which the sermon ends. The approaching divine judgment, he asserts, is "undoubtedly for the daring and presumptuous wickedness of the land." And not the least of "our crying sins" is "carnal mirth and recreation upon ordination and thanksgiving day evenings." The minister had apparently gotten word of a planned celebration later in the day. Cheated by the meetinghouse tragedy out of the customary contests, games, dancing, and further feasting and drinking after the raising fifteen months before, the "young and gay" now looked forward to celebrating their new meetinghouse in proper style on the occasion of the dedication. But not if the town minister would have his way:

My young friends, I desire you would remember that the occasion of our rejoicing this day is of a religious nature, and therefore our joy is to be manifested in religious exercises, and it will be utterly unsuitable to close the day with any kind of carnal mirth and recreation; and, therefore, if you have any of you conceived a purpose of engaging in or carrying on such an unseasonable recreation, you will, I hope, upon serious deliberation, relinquish that purpose. I hope you will consider that if you do not, but will go one with your design, you will hereby bring a reproach upon this town and a grievous scandal upon the Christian profession, and highly offend the great God, and expose your precious and immortal souls, and that this unseasonable exercise will by no means compensate for the evil you will bring upon yourselves thereby.

And here the minister makes his second direct reference to the tragedy at the raising of the frame. "I hope you will not forget," he warns his young listeners, "how you were disappointed in your purposes of such an untimely diversion when the house was raised. I pray you to consider that though that would have been a very unsuitable time for carnal mirth, this will be much more so." Unlike the raising day, devoted to the practical purpose of getting up the frame, the dedication day had been "set . . . apart for religious exercises; to act so directly counter thereto would be a grievous sin against that God to whose service we sanctified the day."[28] Whether his plea and his warning were heeded, the record unfortunately contains not so much as a hint. If it did, we should know much more about the effectiveness of ministerial authority—and about the competing power of country custom and the celebratory urge—than we do. In any case, Mr. Livermore's authority in Wilton was nearing its end, for the "dismission" that was being discussed as a possibility back in 1773 was finally to take place in February 1777.

In assessing the various responses of Wilton and its neighbors to the meetinghouse tragedy, with the intent of discovering some key to the rural culture of the time and region, it is not enough simply to point out the differences among the minister's sermon, the popular ballad, and the superstitions of folklore. Obviously, ideas and sensibilities on all of these cultural levels operated in tension with one another. They were not mutually exclusive, just as the vernacular meetinghouse form excluded neither its folk-derived orientation to the compass nor some embellishments of formal neoclassicism. Most of those who copied and sang the vernacular ballad were at the same time absorbing on a weekly basis the reasoned and anti-dogmatic pronouncements of their learned minister, while the minister himself, after rejecting the providential doctrines of his ancestors in one context, invoked precisely those doctrines in interpreting contemporary public events and in warning against what he perceived as a local social evil. While we can be certain that the minister rejected with scorn and disapproval the folk beliefs in preternatural signs and influences that were a part of the response, it is by no means certain that the majority of the townspeople did so.

And there were other tensions as well, most notably, in a community where church and civic life were blended, the confusion

the family farm and the outward impulse to associate with neighbors and to engage in communal activities, of which the meetinghouse raising was only the most spectacular example.

Finally, it is clear that Wilton and its neighboring communities were joining the rest of the region and much of the rest of British America in paying more attention, for the moment, to the immediate future than to the past. By dedication day, the meetinghouse frame had collapsed fifteen months before. The dead, while certainly not forgotten, had been buried. The bereaved had gotten on with their lives. The injured, with a few exceptions, had recovered. The meetinghouse, the town's central civic project for several years, was now completed; the arguments, the frustrations, the problems, the delays, the worries over finance, even the tragedy were now behind. What lay ahead was more compelling. Militia companies were being reorganized and reinvigorated, townsmen were joining committees of correspondence, their province assembly was on the point of being dissolved and a provincial congress formed in its stead. News of the outside world, especially from occupied Boston and their own turmoiled capital of Portsmouth, took on a new and ever-increasing importance. No one could have predicted precisely that Lexington and Concord lay but three months ahead, but ominous signs of coming conflict were everywhere, affecting even something as profoundly local as the relationship between Wilton and its minister.

If the nineteenth-century historians of Wilton were right, the troubles between Mr. Livermore and the community that finally ended his pastorate at the age of forty-eight stemmed from political disagreements over the Revolution. This could hardly have been the whole reason, since some sort of trouble had been brewing at least since 1773 and since there is no evidence that the minister was an overt Loyalist. In fact, he lived peacefully in the community, on good terms with his former parishioners and his ministerial successors and occasionally supplying the pulpit there and elsewhere, until he died in 1809. Perhaps, though, the dedication sermon of 1775, expressing both a horror of "civil" war and a stern judgment of certain aspects of the youth culture of the day, suggests a growing generational incompatibility between the conservative social values of the minister and the political and social inclinations of the majority. If this was the case, a state of actual revolutionary warfare could well have been the catalyst that brought to a breaking point tensions in the official relationship between pastor and people.[30]

Thus the horrible events of September 1773 are less visible through the veil of Revolutionary fervor and anticipation that soon engulfed the community—and their meaning less clear—than we wish. Certainly there were important responses on three cultural levels, the folk, the popular, and the learned. Certainly all of these responses, taken together, reveal a mixed mentality, an amalgam of superstition, folklore, vernacular tradition, a regional religious heritage, and a modernized theology. They also reveal a society struggling with change and the consciousness of impending danger. Through all of this, however, the memory of the meetinghouse tragedy, veiled though it was in some of its details, stayed alive for several generations, perpetuated in oral tradition, scribal transmission, and public consciousness. Every community needs a story. For the story of Wilton, it was this awful event that was claimed by subsequent generations as its one distinctive element, the keystone in building a town's communal memory.

Appendixes

News Accounts of the Wilton Disaster

I.

Extract of a letter from New-Ipswich, Sept. 13, 1773.

Last Tuesday the most melancholy accident of the kind, happened at Wilton, in New-Hampshire Government, that perhaps has been known in the Country: A large company was collected there to raise a Meeting-House, and they got up the body of it, the beams and joists, and on these had a large quantity of boards for the more immediate convenient standing; they had also raised part of the roof, in doing which they had occasion for a number of crowbars and axes, which rested on the building while the people got together, and were in the act of raising another double pair of principals with a king-post, when on a sudden the beam broke at the mortice in the middle, by which upwards of fifty persons fell to the bottom of the house, with the timber, bars, axes, &c. and exhibited a scene to the astonished spectators around the house (for there were no persons in the bottom of it, all having withdrawn through fear of what might happen) which cannot be described; and could only be equalled by the blood and brains, shrieks and groans of the dead and wounded, which were immediately seen and heard. Three were killed outwright; another survived but a short time, and several others have since died of their wounds. Of fifty-three that fell, not one escaped without broken bones, terrible bruises or wounds from the axes, &c. And as they were men picked up from that and neighboring towns, and many of them heads of families, the news of their catastrophe filled those places with weeping, lamentation and woe, and may fully mind us that "Man knoweth not his time," but "at such an hour as we think not the son of Man cometh," and it therefore concerns us to be always ready.

Belonging to Wilton

Killed instantly. George Laney

Mortally wounded. Francis Putnam and Ebenezer Coster (both expected to be dead before this Time).

Wounded. Joseph Parker, Joseph Stiles, Isaac Frye, Oliver Holte, Jacob Adams, Fiefield Holte, Alexander Mulliken [*sic*], Samuel Mulliken [*sic*], Joseph Putnam, Archelaus Putnam Jr., John Stevens, John Cram Jr., Simeon Riggs, and Benjamin————.

Belonging to New-Ipswich

Killed instantly. Simeon Fletcher

Wounded. John Datten, Simeon Rite, Francis Fletcher, William Clary, Joseph Tucker, Daniel Stratton, and Elijah Flagg.

Belonging to Temple

Wounded. Peter Brown, Benjamin Crayon, Nathaniel Shattuck, Joseph Foster, Isaac Brewer, and Stephen Lander.

Belonging to Lyndeborough

Killed instantly. Reuben Stiles.

Mortally wounded. Joseph Suerance, Timothy Calton, and Benjamin Jones; the first died the next Day, the second lived but four Days, and the third is supposed to be since dead.

Belonging to Andover

Wounded. Joseph Blanchard and Joshua Chandler.

Belonging to Miles-Slip

Wounded. Daniel Parker and Stephen Blanchard.

Abel Blanchard of Mason, John Blanchard of New Concord, James Maconey of Pepperrell, and Ephraim Barber of Stratham were also wounded.

> *Massachusetts Gazette and Weekly News-Letter, September 13, 1773*
> *Boston Evening-Post, September 20, 1773 (Without names)*
> *New-Hampshire Gazette, September 24, 1773*
> *Boston Gazette and Country Journal, September 27, 1773 (With the addition of eleven "wounded" from Lyndeborough)*
> *Connecticut Courant, September 28, 1773 (Without names)*

II.

We learn from Wilton, in New Hampshire, that on Tuesday last, as a great number of Persons were assisting in raising the Frame of a new Meeting House in that Town, one of the large beams accidentally fell, by which means four of the Men were instantly killed, and 49 wounded, two or three of whom are since dead, and it was tho't several others of them could not recover.

> *Boston Evening-Post, September 13, 1773*
> *Massachusetts Gazette and Boston Post-Boy & Advertiser,*
> *September 16, 1773*
> *Connecticut Gazette, September 17, 1773*
> *Providence Gazette, September 18, 1773*
> *Pennsylvania Journal, September 22, 1773*

III.

We hear from a Place called Wilton, in New-Hampshire Government, that on Tuesday last, as a great Number of People were assisting to raise a Meeting-House the king post gave way, when [line missing]ty one Persons; together with the greatest Part of the Frame fell to the Ground, by which Accident four Men were killed on the Spot, three died of their Bruises the next day, and many others it is feared cannot recover.

> *Massachusetts Gazette and Boston Post-Boy & Advertiser,*
> *September 13, 1773*

IV.

On Tuesday se'ennight, as a great number of people were assisting in raising the frame of a new meeting house in Wilton, New-Hampshire, one of the large beams accidentally gave way, when the greatest part of the frame, with 53 persons that were upon it, fell to the ground, by which unhappy event, three men were instantly killed, and fifty wounded, two of whom have since died of their wounds, and four more are thought to be past recovery. This accident has put by the raising for the present.

> *Massachusetts Spy, September 16, 1773*
> *Pennsylvania Gazette, September 29, 1773*

V.

The 7th Instant, being the Day appointed for raising a new Meeting-House in Wilton, 60 by 45 Feet, 27 Feet Post; 120 Men were pitch'd upon to perform the Business, which they design'd to accomplish in nine Hours, and had almost compleated the same by three o'Clock in the Afternoon, when a most shocking and melancholly Accident happened in the following Manner, viz. The Shore which was put under the middle Beam to strengthen it, while the King Post and Spars of the Roof were fixing, gave Way, and 60 Men fell, when three were instantly kill'd, and a fourth soon after died of his Wounds. Above 50 of the 60 are kill'd and wounded, some with broken Legs, Arms, &c. and 'tis expected a Number more will not live.

Since the foregoing Account we hear five more are dead.

We expected before the publication of this Paper, a more particular Account of the above Accident, would have been sent, with the Names of the kill'd and wounded, but it being neglected, can give no better than the foregoing.

The following is said to be the Names of those that died first, Coaster, Chandler, Caldwell, two Millikens, Wiggins, and Hutchison.

New-Hampshire Gazette, September 17, 1773

Corrected Casualty List

WILTON, KILLED

George Lancey

WILTON, INJURED

Jacob Adams
Ebenezer Coster
John Cram, Jr.
Isaac Frye
Fifield Holt
Oliver Holt
Alexander Milliken [Jr.][1]
Samuel Milliken[1]

Josiah Parker
Archelaus Putnam[2]
Francis Putnam
Joseph Putnam
Simeon Riggs
John Stevens
Joseph Stiles

LYNDEBOROUGH, KILLED

Timothy Carlton (or Carleton)
Reuben Stiles

Joseph Severance

LYNDEBOROUGH, INJURED

Edward Bevins[3]
Thomas Boffee
David Carlton (or Carleton)

Jonathan Chamberlain [Jr.][4]
Uriah Cram
Ebenezer Gardner

Note: Unless otherwise indicated, all towns are in New Hampshire.

1. Also spelled Mullikan. Alexander and Samuel were brothers. It is possible, though unlikely, that the Alexander Milliken who was the victim was the father of these two rather than one of the brothers.

2. Listed as "Jr." in the newspaper casualty list, but he appears to have been the son of Jacob Putnam, the first permanent settler in Wilton.

3. Also spelled Bevens and Bevings.

Nehemiah Hutchinson
Benjamin Jones
John Rowe

Benjamin Senter
Andrew Thompson

New Ipswich, Killed

Simeon Fletcher

New Ipswich, Injured

William Clary (or McClary)
John Dutton
Elijah Flagg
Francis Fletcher

William Spear
Daniel Stratton
Joseph Tucker
Simeon Wright

Temple, Injured

Isaac Brewer
Peter Brown
Benjamin Cragin

Joshua Foster
Stephen Saunders [5]
Nathaniel Shattuck

Mile Slip (later Milford), Injured

Stephen Blanchard

Daniel Parker

Andover, Mass., Injured

Joseph Blanchard

Joshua Chandler

Other Injured

Ephraim Barker, Stratham
or Amherst
Abel [or Abiel] Blanchard,
Mason

John Blanchard, New Concord
(later Washington)
James Maconey [Mahoney?],
Pepperrell, Mass.

---

4. This victim could have been Jonathan Chamberlain, Sr., as indicated in the index of Donovan's and Woodward's *History of Lyndeborough*. However, since at the time of the accident the senior Chamberlain was sixty-three, substantially older than any of the casualties whose ages are known, it seems much more likely that the victim was his twenty-nine-year-old son, Jonathan.

5. Also spelled Sanders.

The Ballad

POLLY LEWIS–PHEBE HOWARD VERSION	ASA BLACK VERSION
	An Elegy upon the fall of 53 Men, at Wilton September ye 17 1773
(Untitled)	

1.

Attention give and you shall hear
A melancholy theme
Tis such an instance as there is
But very seldom seen

1.

Attention give and you shall hear
a melancholly theme
tis such an instance as there is
but very sildom scen

2.

In seventeen Hundred seventy
   three
September seventh Day
At Wilton did Almity God
His anger there Display

2.

In Seventeen hundred Seventy
   three
September Seventeenth Day
At Wilton did almity God
his anger their [sic] display

3.

Of men a Great Collection met
A meeting house to raise
Herein to speak gods holy word
And for to sing his praise

3.

Of Men a great Collection Meet
A Meeting house to Raise
Wherein to speak Gods holy word
and for to sing his Praise

4.

God did there Labour prosper in
Erecting of that fraim
Untill it was almost compleat
And joyfull they became

4.

God Did their Labour prosper in
Errectin of this fraim
untill it was almost Compleat
and joyfull they became

5.

they thought the worst was past
   and gone
they were both bold and brave

5.

they thought the worst was past
   and gone
and they were bold and brave

poor souls they did but little think
they were so nigh there graves

poor souls they did but little think
that were so near their grave

6.

All on a Sudden a beam broak
it let down fifty three
full twenty seven feet they fell
a shocking sight to see

6.

All on a Suden a beme broke
and let down fifty three
full twenty seven feet they fell
a mournfull sight to see

7.

Much timber with these men
    did fall
and Eged tools likewise
all in a heap together Lay
With bitter Shrieks and Cries

7.

Much timber with these men did
    fall
And edged tools Likewise
All in a heap together Lay
With bitter screcks [?] and cries

8.

It would pierce the hardest heart
    to hear
the bitter Cries and grones
of them that in the ruins Lay
with wounds and broaken bones

8.

Twould Pierce the Hardest Heart
    to hear
the Sighs and Bitter groans
Of those that in the Ruins Lay
With Wounds and Broken bones

9.

some lay with broken sholder
    bones
and some with broken arms
Others with broken legs and
    thies
and divers other harms

9.

Some Lay with broken Shoulder
    Bones
and some with broken Arms
Others with Broken Legs and
    thighs
and Divers other harms

10.

Many lay bleeding on the ground
all barth'd in crimson gore
Crying dear Jesus mighty to save
thy mercy we implore

10.

Many lay Bleeding on the ground
All Bathed in Crimson gore
Crying Dear Jesus Mighty to Save
thy Mercy we Implore

11.

Hearts piersing sight for to
    behold
which caused many a sob
to see these poor distresed men
Ly waloing in their blood

11.

Hear the peirceing sight for to
    behold
it Caused Many a sob
to see these poor Distressed Men
Lay wallowing in their Blood

12.

One in an instantly was kild
his soul has taken flight
to Mantions of Eternal day
or everlasting night

12.

One instantaneously was Kill'd
his Soul has taken flight
to Mansions of Eternal Day
or Everlasting Night

13.

two more in a few moments
    Spent
did bid this world adieu
wich are rejected of their god
or with his Chosen few

13.

Two Two [*sic*] More in a few
    Minutes Space
Did bid this world adue
Which are Rejected of their god,
or with his Cosen [*sic*] few

14.

two more in a Short time did
    pass
threw death dark shady vail
which now are in the realmns
    [*sic*] of Joy
or the infernal Hell

14.

Two More in a few Short time
    Did pass
through Deaths Dark Shady Vail
Which are Now In the Realms
    of Joy
or in the Infernal Hell

15.

but we must hope their precious
    Souls
are with their Saviour dear
reeping the fruites the blessed
    frutes
of faithful Servants here

15.

But We Must hope their precious
    Souls
are with their Jesus Dear
Reaping the frutes the blessed
    fruits
of faithfull Servents here

16.

And if this be their happy Case
Glory to god be given
O blessed day, o happy fall
that Sent there Souls to heaven

16.

And If this be their hapy Case
Glory to god be given
O blessed day o happy fall
that Sent their Souls to heaven

17.

Where theres no danger of a fall

and nothing to molest
no care no grief for to desturb
their ever lasting rest

17.

Wheir there is No Danger of a
    fall
Nor Nothing to Molest
No grief No Sorrow to Disturb
their Everlasting Rest

18.

While their dear friends are
   bowed down
with Sorrow for there Sake
Grieving and mourning til there
   hearts
are ready for to brake

19.

Widows ware garments of Saccloth
There grief is very great
they mourning go like turtle doves
When they have left their mate

20.

Children of fathers are bereft
they mourn like little lambs
When they have bin engag'd
   in play
and lost Sight of there dams

21.

Fathers for there deceased sons
go mourning all the day
but blessed be the name of god

that gives and takes away

22.

poor tender hearted mothers are

with Sorrow bowed down
the Children which their bodies
   bare
are now made meet for worms

23.

Brothers and Sisters follow'd have

there Corpses to the grave
and bid to them a long fairwell
and took of them their leave

18.

While their Dear friend are
   bowed Down
With Sorrows for their sake
Grieving and Morning till their
   Hearts
are Ready for to Brake

18. [number repeated]

Fathers for their Disceased Sones
go Mourning all the Day
but blessed be the Name of god
that gives and takes Away

19.

Poor tender hearted Mothers are
With Sorrows bowed Down
the Children which their bodys
   Bare
are Now Made Meat for worms

21. [no number 20]

Children of Fathers are bereft
they Mourn like Little lambs
when they have been Engaged In
   play
and lost Sight of their Dams

22.

Widows wear Garments of Sack
   cloth
their Griefs are Very great
they Mourning go Like turtle
   Doves
When they have Lost their Mates

23.

Brothers and Sisters followed
   have
their Corpses to the Grave
and bid to them a Long fare well
And took of them their Leave

24.

and now who ere doth read
    these lines
and meditate there on
their hearts will melt if they
    are not
as hard as any Stone

24.

We have seen our fellows Called
    away
in to Eternity
Which is a Sertain Evidence

of our Motality

25.

Remember well the mournfull
    Scean
and melancholy day
in which the almighty Sent grim
    death
and took there Souls away

25.

And Now Who Ere Does Read
    these lines
and Meditates their on
their hearts would brake if they
    were not
as hard as any Stone

26.

To the Eternal unseen world

to Spend Eternity
of un [sic] expressed felissety

or boundless misery

26.

Remember Well that Mournful
    Seen
that Melancholly Day
In Which the Almighty Sent grim
    death
to Snatch their Souls away

27.

according as their works have bin
in this vinyard of the Lord
So they receive of god there Judg
there right and just reward

Improvement / Improvment

27.

Into the unseen Eaternal world
to Spend Eternity
of unexpressed felicety
or bound less Misery

28.

according as their Works have
    been
In the vinyards of their Lord
So they will Receive of god their
    Judge
their Right and Just Reward

28.

But let us Some improvment
    make
and to our Selves apply
this awfull providence of god
that Comes to us so nigh

Application

29.

We have Seen our fellows Call'd
    away

29.

Come Let us sum Improvements
    Make

into eternity
Which is a Certain evidence
of our mortallaty

and to our Selves apply
this Awful providence of God
that Comes to us Nigh

30.

by it we See and Certain be
our lives uncertain are
therefore let all boath great
    and Small
for Sudden death prepair

30.

By this we See and Certain be
our lives uncertain are
therefore Let all both great and
    Small
for Suden Death prepare

31.

for at gods Call we marst [?] to
When death doth give the blow
We must apear at his Comemand
Whether prepard or no

31.

For at God Call We all Must Bow
When Death Does give the Blow
We Must appear at his Command
Wheather prepared or No

32.

When grim death with his gashly
    eyes
Shall in our faces Stair
and Summons us for to appear
at gods tribunal bar

32.

When grim Death with his gashly
    Eyes
Shall in our faces Stare
and Summons us for to appear
at gods tribunal bar

33.

We must Submit we cant
    withstand
the messenger of death
We must with cold and
    Trembling Lips
resign our vital breath

33.

We Must Submit we Canot with
    Stand
the Messenger of Death
We Must with Cold & trembling
    Lips
Resign our vital Breath

34.

And lanch into an unseen world

to meet Omnipotence
to have our doom pronouns'd
    and to
recieve our recompence

34.

And Lanch Into the u[n]scen
    worlds
to Meet omnipotence
to have our Doom pronounced
    and too
Receive our Recompence

35.

And if our deeds have evil been

35.

And if our Deeds have Evil been

We Shall recieve this doom	we Shall Receive this Doom
depart from me I know you not	Depart from me I Know you not
for you did me disown	for you Did me Disone

36.

Down Down into a deep abiss	Down Down into a Deep abyss
of wo and misery	of woe and Misery
our Souls are plung'd there to	our Souls are plungd therein to
remain	Dwell
throughout eternity	through out Eternity

37.

an Angry god is pouring forth	An Angry God is pouring forth
the vials of his wrath	the Vials of his Wrath
and indignation upon us	his Indignation upon us
Which is the Second death	Which is the Second Death

38.

Therefore as we must all be Judg'd	Therefor as we must all be judgd
according as we have done	According as weve Done
tis highly needfull for us all	tis highly Needful for us all
the Christian race to run	the Christian Race to Run

39.

Put on brest plates of	Put On breasts plates of
Righteousness	Righteousness
and take the Shield of faith	And take the Sheild of faith
the Spirits Sword for to defend	And the Spirit Sword for to Defend
us in the narrow path	us in the Narrow path

40.

Let us be making peace with god	Let us be Making peace with God
while we have life and breath	While we have Life and breath
that so we may prepaired be	that So we May prepared be
to met a Sudden death	to Meet a Sudden Death

41.

And be there by translated from	And be thereby translated from
a world of misery	A World of Misery
into a world of joy and bliss	Into a world of Joy and Bliss
to dwell with god on high	to Dwell with God on high

42.

To drink of the Clear Streams
   of Joy
that flow at gods right hand
and to injoy his heavenly Love
for ever without end

43.

That this may be our happy Case
When we this life do end
god grant of his Infinite grace
threw Jesus Christ Amen

42.

To Drink of those Clear Streams
   of Joy
that flow at Gods Right hand
And to Enjoy his heavenly Love
forever without End

43.

That this May be our happy Case
When we this Life Do End
God Grant of his infinite Grace
Through Jesus Christ Amen

THE BOSTON BROADSIDE OF 1818

(THE BALLAD'S FIRST KNOWN APPEARANCE IN PRINT)

WILTON TRAGEDY

Attention give, and you shall hear
 A melancholy theme;
'Tis such an instance as there is
 But very seldom seen.

In seventeen hundred seventy three,
 September seventh day,
At Wilton the Almighty God
 His anger did display.

Of men a great collection met,
 A Meeting–House to raise,
Wherein to speak God's holy word,
 And for to sing his Praise.

God did their labour prosper, in
 Erecting of this Frame,
Until it was almost complete
 And joyful they became.

They thought the worst was past and gone
 And they were bold and brave.
Poor souls they did but little think
 They were so near the grave.

But on a sudden a beam broke,
 And let down fifty-three,
Full twenty-seven feet they fell,
 A shocking sight to see.

Much timber with these men did fall,
 And edged tools likewise,
All in a heap together lay,
 With bitter shrieks and cries.

Many lay bleeding on the ground,
 All bath'd in crimson gore,
Crying dear Jesus, mightily to save,
 Thy mercy we implore.

Heart piercing sight for to behold;
 It caused many a sob
To see these poor distressed men
 Lay wallowing in their blood.

One instantaneously was kill'd;
 His soul has taken flight
To mansions of eternal day,
 Or everlasting night.

Two more in a few minute's space
 Did bid this world adieu;
Who are rejected of their God,
 Or with his chosen few.

Two more in a short time did pass
 Through Death's dark shady vale;
And to the pleasing scenes below,
 Have bid a long farewell.

But we must hope their precious souls
 Are with their Saviour dear,
Reaping the fruits, the happy fruits
 Of faithful servants here.

And if this be their happy case,
 Glory to God be given;
O! blessed day, O! happy fall
 That sent their souls to Heaven.

Where there's no danger of a fall
 And nothing to molest;
No care, nor grief for to disturb
 Their everlasting rest.

Whilst their dear friends [page torn, illeg.] bowed
 With sorrow for their [page torn, illeg.]
Grieving and mourning [page torn, illeg.]
 Are ready for to break.

Widows wear garments of sack cloth,
    Their sorrows they are great [end punctuation illeg.]
They mourning go like turtle doves
    When they have lost their mates.

Children of fathers are bereft,
    They mourn like little lambs
That are by some unhappy stroke,
    Bereaved of their dams.

Fathers for their deceased sons
    Go mourning all the day;
But blessed be the name of God
    Who gives and takes away.

Poor tender hearted mothers are,
    With sorrows bowed down,
Those children which their bodies bare,
    Are now made meat for worms.

Brothers and sisters follow'd have,
    Their corpses to the Grave;
And bade to them a long farewell,
    And took of them their leave.

One maiden lover is bereft
    Of him she held most dear;
And for the loss of her true love
    She sheds a pearly tear.

And now whoe'er does read these lines
    And meditate thereon;
Their hearts will melt if they are not
    As hard as any stone.

Remember well that mournful scene,
    And melancholy day,
In which th'Almighty sent grim death
    And snatch'd their souls away.

Into th'unseen eternal world,
    To meet omnipotence;
To hear their doom pronounc'd, and to
    Receive their recompense.

Therefore as we must all be judg'd
    According as we've done;
'Tis highly needful for us all
    The Christian life to run.

Put on breast plates of Righteousness,
    And take the shield of faith;
The spirit's sword for our defence,
    Along the narrow path.

Let us be making peace with God
    While we have life and breath;
That so we may prepared b
    To meet a sudden death.

And be thereby translated from
    A world of misery
Into a world of joy and bliss,
    To dwell with God on high.

To drink of those pure streams of joy,
    Which flow at God's right hand;
And to enjoy his Heavenly love
    Forever without end.

That this may be our happy case
    When we this life shall end;
God grant of his infinite Grace,
    Through Jesus Christ, Amen.

Printed for N. Coverly, Milk-Street

Possible Tunes [1]

At some time during its currency, the ballad responding to the Wilton meetinghouse tragedy was sung. Conventional wisdom, of course, assumes that ballads by definition are and were set to music, though there is now some doubt in scholarly circles that this was invariably the case. As for the meetinghouse ballad, however, two nineteenth-century historians, one of Wilton and the other of New Ipswich, testify to its perpetuation for a time in song. The author and singers of the ballad had two sources upon which to draw for an appropriate tune. One was the ballad tradition of British folklore. The other was New England psalm singing.

In order for a tune to work with these verses, it had to be written in what was called "common meter." That means there had to be four lines, or musical phrases, the first and third having four "beats," or emphases, and the second and fourth three. As applied to psalm and hymn tunes, this meter was usually described by counting syllables rather than beats, resulting in this descriptive notation: 8.6.8.6. As the term suggests, "common meter" tunes in the seventeenth and eighteenth century British world were probably more numerous than most other kinds. "Common meter," however, was often doubled, resulting in an 8.6.8.6.8.6.8.6 (or 14.14.14.14) pattern rather than one half that size. In order for the Wilton ballad to be sung to an eight-line or eight-phrase tune such as that, two stanzas would have to be sung as a unit, since the melody of the eighth line was usually a variation on, rather than a duplication of, the fourth. Obviously, the ballad was not intended to be sung that way; the stanzas are not paired, and most versions contain an odd number of verses. It was necessary, therefore, to use a four-phrase common meter tune, diagramed musically either ABAC or ABCD.

The most ubiquitous such tune in the British ballad tradition was probably some version of "Chevy Chase," a sixteenth-century air origi-

---

1. This discussion is intended to be suggestive only, and certainly not definitive. It is based largely on *Music in Colonial Massachusetts*, a two-volume collection of papers from a conference held by the Colonial Society of Massachusetts in 1973, edited by Barbara Lambert and published by the Society in 1980 and 1985; an examination of several editions of the *Bay Psalm Book* (*The Psalms, Hymns, and Spiritual Songs of the Old and New Testaments: Faithfully Translated into English Metre*); and a letter from and brief but helpful conversation with Arthur F. Schrader.

nally associated with a tragic ballad arising from the English-Scottish border wars and subsequently applied with great frequency to both English and Anglo-American broadside ballads. Among the ballads probably set to that tune or one very much like it was a mournful response to the murder of two English children entitled "The Children in the Woods" or "The Babes in the Wood," which was extremely popular in the eighteenth century on both sides of the Atlantic. Eventually in some sections, that ballad acquired at least two separate tunes of its own, one called "The Babes in the Wood" and the other "Now Ponder Well" (the first line of the ballad), which could easily have been known in New England. Another well-known tune that would have worked was a Scottish folk song called "The Broom, the Bonny Broom," which has been speculatively matched to a 1773 Boston execution ballad, "The Dying Groans of Levi Ames."

If the ballad singers decided to reach into their sacred rather than their secular tradition, they found an even greater variety of musical possibilities. Among the common meter standards in the psalter used by most New Englanders were "St. David's Tune," used for the New England version of Psalm 95 ("O come let us unto the Lord / Shout forth with joyful noise"); "Low Dutch," which performed the same service for, among others, Psalm 23 ("The Lord to me a shepherd is / Want therefore shall not I"); and a large handful of others, including "Martyrs," "York," "Oxford," and "Litchfield." Possibly the rural singers had also been exposed to the hymn tunes of Isaac Watts, who was composing early in the century, and of New England's own William Billings, who had only recently begun. If rural New Hampshire congregations had by 1773 accepted any of the Watts hymns into their worship as an alternative to traditional psalm-singing, the most eligible tune for the Wilton ballad might have been "St. Anne," probably composed by William Croft in 1708, to which Watts fitted "Our God, our help in ages past / Our hope for years to come."

APPENDIX E

Glossary of Building Terms

Adze	A tool somewhat resembling an axe, except that the blade is narrower, slightly curved, and fixed at right angles to the handle. Used for smoothing hewn surfaces.
Auger	A twisting tool for boring holes, often used in combination with a chisel to make mortises.
Bark spud	A long-handled tool with a flat blade on the end for peeling bark from logs.
Bent	Section of a building frame, usually a pair of posts connected by a girt.
Box pew	In a church or meetinghouse, an enclosed seating area usually fitted with hinged benches. In early New England, most often owned individually and designed for occupancy by the owner's family.
Broad axe	Axe with a relatively broad blade, in the eighteenth century beveled on one side only (like a chisel) in order to produce a straight side when hewing a log.
Broadside	The complete frame of one side of a building, raised as a unit.
Chisel	A straight cutting tool in any of various forms and sizes, usually with a wooden handle, designed for cutting holes or openings in wood. The workman ordinarily held the chisel in place with one hand while using a hammer or mallet to drive it with the other.
Common rafter	In a roof supported by both principal and common rafters, one of several single rafters inserted in pairs at intervals between the principal rafters and supported at its middle by a purlin. Important mainly as a support

for the roof boards rather than as a structural unit in the frame as a whole. Also called a "spar."

Double rafter · A rafter, usually a principal rafter, consisting of two roughly parallel timbers, one below the other, connected by short struts.

Felling axe · A heavy axe whose blade is beveled on both sides to produce a knife edge, intended mainly for felling trees.

Gallery · In a meetinghouse, an interior projecting balcony for seating at second-story level.

Gin pole · A single pole fixed temporarily in place and fitted with block and tackle to aid in raising or lifting.

Girders · Heavy timbers connecting the sills of a building, to which floor joists are attached.

Girts · Timbers running horizontally along the frame between the posts, usually about halfway between sill and plate.

Joists · The horizontal timbers supporting the floor of the building, either the ground floor or one above. *See* Sleeper.

King post · In a roof truss of this design, the vertical member suspended from the apex of a pair of rafters and supporting the center of the tie beam that spans the building at the feet of the rafters.

Mortise · In the most common form of joint, a rectangular hole or pocket in a timber designed to receive the tenon of the piece to which it is joined.

Long pew · Term used by the Wilton building committee to refer to an unenclosed benchlike pew. Also called "slip pew."

Pike pole · A long pole tipped with a metal point, used in raising sections of the frame.

Plate · A horizontal timber connecting the top of the posts of a frame. The beams and rafters rest atop the plate.

Porch	In a meetinghouse, an enclosed exterior stairway to the gallery.
Post	One of the main vertical supports of the frame, running between sill and plate.
Prick post	A post other than a corner post on a gable end of the building.
Principal rafter	One of the rafters, sometimes doubled, that is part of one of the main trusses of the building, thus playing a role in holding the frame together as well as supporting the roof.
Pulpit window	In a meetinghouse, the window immediately behind the raised pulpit, at an intermediate level between the ground floor and the gallery.
Purlin	A comparatively light horizontal timber connecting the rafters and sometimes acting as a support for the roof boards.
Queen post	In a roof truss of this design, one of two vertical posts resting on the tie beam and supporting a rafter. The Wilton meetinghouse was built with king posts instead.
Rabbet	A groove in a board or plank designed to receive the end or the edge of an adjoining member.
Ridgepole	The topmost horizontal member of the building, connecting the peaks of the rafters.
Scribe	To mark out both (or all) parts of each joint of the frame individually; to mark one member to be cut to fit snugly against an adjoining member.
Shears	A lifting device consisting of a stationary and a moveable pole, the two joined near the bottom of both and operated by rope, block, and tackle. (*Cf.* gin pole.)
Sheathing	The covering of the frame; the fabric of the building. In the eighteenth century, usually composed of inch-thick rough-sawn boards. The sheathing was usually covered with clapboards.

Shore   Any temporary supporting device. At the Wilton meet-
                 inghouse raising, a post used to support a tie beam un-
                 til it could be joined to the king post.

Sill   The heavy horizontal timbers atop the foundation
                 upon which the building rests.

Sleeper   Another name for joist, especially a ground-floor joist.

Sounding board   In a meetinghouse, a hardwood structure over the pul-
                 pit intended to reflect and amplify the speaker's voice.
                 Sometimes called a "canopy."

Spar   Another name for common rafter.

Stud   In post and beam construction, one of the several rel-
                 atively light vertical members dispersed between the
                 posts, connecting sill and girt and girt and plate, play-
                 ing some structural role but intended mainly as sup-
                 port for the sheathing.

Tenon   The projection to be inserted into the mortise of an
                 adjoining member to form a joint, usually secured by
                 pinning. Some types of tenon had special names—in-
                 cluding teazle, tusk, soffit, or dovetail—designating a
                 particular shape or function.

Tie beam   One of the large horizontal timbers across the top of
                 the frame, usually associated with a pair of opposing
                 posts and, with a set of rafters above it, forming the
                 bottom of a roof truss.

Truss   A framework of rafters, tie beam, king post or queen
                 posts, and auxiliary members, forming one of the prin-
                 cipal supports of the roof.

Twibil   A double-bladed hatchet-like tool used for cutting
                 mortises.

Vendue   An auction. In Wilton, a method of awarding contracts
                 to supply materials for the meetinghouse by bidding,
                 the contract going to the low bidder.

Wall plate   *See* Plate.

Notes

❧ ❧

Chapter 1. Wilton

1. *New Hampshire Gazette*, September 17, 1773.

2. *Provincial and State Papers of New Hampshire* 10 (1877), p. 631.

3. "Fall of the Wilton N.H. Meeting House," *New England Historical and Genealogical Register* [hereafter *NEHGR*] 22 (1868), p. 235; *The History of New Ipswich, From Its First Grant in MDCCXXXVI to the Present Time* (Boston: Gould & Lincoln, 1852), pp. 155, 256.

4. *The History of New Ipswich* describes a meetinghouse raising in that town in 1812: "Every body in town was present, and great numbers from the neighboring towns. Great jollity and frolic was kept up during the three days; booths were erected, and toddy and punch were dealt out with a profusion that would be deemed scandalous in these days [1852] of temperance pledges" (p. 159).

5. Abiel Livermore and Sewall Putnam, *History of the Town of Wilton, Hillsborough County, New Hampshire* (Lowell, Mass.: Marden & Rowell, 1888), p. 60.

6. Livermore and Putnam, *History of Wilton*, pp. 21–27, 32–37. For the name of Wilton, see Elmer Munson Hunt, *New Hampshire Town Names* (Peterborough, N.H.: Noone House, [1971]), pp. 157–8, which also acknowledges another possibility: Wilton House, estate of the ninth Earl of Pembroke, after whom Wentworth had named Pembroke, New Hampshire, three years earlier. It might lend weight to the latter theory that Wiltshire, in which Wilton House was located, was one of the three English counties that furnished the leadership of the settlement of Andover, Massachusetts, in the early 1640s, and Pembroke was one of the three New Hampshire towns, along with Wilton and Concord, to which the bulk of Andover's emigrés migrated in the 1740s. Philip J. Greven, Jr., *Four Generations: Population, Land, and Family in Colonial Andover, Massachusetts* (Ithaca: Cornell University Press, 1970), pp. 42, 213–14.

7. Charles E. Clark, *The Eastern Frontier: The Settlement of Northern New England, 1610–1763* (New York: Alfred A. Knopf, 1970), pp. 182–83, 199–225; Sumner Chilton Powell, *Puritan Village: The Formation of a New England Town* (Middletown, Conn.: Wesleyan University Press, 1963), pp. 6–11, figs. 1–4 between pp. 44 and 45; David Grayson Allen,

In English Ways: The Movement of Societies and the Transferral of English Local Law and Custom to Massachusetts Bay in the Seventeenth Century (Chapel Hill: University of North Carolina Press for the Institute of Early American History and Culture, 1981), pp. 46, 61–66. In Andover, whence many of the second group of settlers had come, the "open field" system, beginning with the allocation of home lots, is precisely the way the distribution of land was ordered in the 1640s. By the 1660s, however, this method of settlement had been superseded by dispersed farms, the size of which diminished gradually in succeeding generations. Greven, *Four Generations*, pp. 42–71, 224.

8. Clark, *Eastern Frontier*, pp. 198, 214–16.

9. *State Papers of New Hampshire* 38 (1896), pp. 450–53.

10. See Darrett B. Rutman, "People in Process: The New Hampshire Towns of the Eighteenth Century," *Journal of Urban History* 1 (1974–75), p. 282. Wilton's population density in 1773 was 23.2 per square mile, a density suggesting the likelihood of substantial further growth, according to Rutman's findings. If each of Wilton's 121 "polls" was the head of a single-family household, the town had 132 available acres for each such family, more than twice the optimum. The assumption of 121 households yields an average family size of 4.8, smaller than the average eighteenth-century family but perhaps not surprising, since Wilton's population was made up predominantly of young and still growing families. It seems likely, however, that at least a few white males over twenty-one were as yet unmarried and therefore lived under someone else's roof. If we apply the standard 5.7 persons per household used by many demographers, there would have been only 102 households, or one for each 157 acres, roughly three times the optimum.

11. Technically, the grant in 1749 to the various proprietors of Wilton, with its provision for the meetinghouse lot and town common, was through Joseph Blanchard of Andover, the proprietors' representative to whom the Masonian Proprietors granted the township. *Town Papers of New Hampshire* 9 (1875), p. 794.

12. Abiel Abbot, *History of Andover from Its Settlement to 1829* (Andover, Mass.: Flagg and Gould, 1829), p. 181. The Andover settlers were members of Philip Greven's "fourth generation," which was marked by extensive emigration to other places in New England, especially to three of the new towns in New Hampshire. Greven, *Four Generations*, pp. 212–14.

13. Locations of roads and farms are based on a composite map derived from a base map of 1775, printed in the *Wilton Journal*, September 28, 1950, a supplemental hand-drawn map for 1763 held by the Wilton Historical Society, and location by range and lot number of various families discussed in the genealogical section of Livermore and Putnam, *History of Wilton*.

14. Wilton Town Records (ms., New Hampshire State Archives, Concord), p. 60.

15. Wilton Town Records, pp. 102, 129.

16. A New Hampshire census of 1773 counted 580 "inhabitants" in Wilton and 121 "polls," or taxable resident men above the age of twenty-one. Evarts B. Greene and Virginia D. Harrington, *American Population Before the Federal Census of 1790* (New York: Columbia University Press, 1932; repr. Gloucester, Mass.: Peter Smith, 1966), p. 79.

17. Livermore and Putnam, *History of Wilton*, pp. 47–48. Using the 1773 population of 580, this works out to just under four percent of the population who filled important leadership posts in that twelve-year period. While comparable figures for New England towns vary considerably, this would not have been an atypical percentage (though the percentages ranged from 1.5 to 15.2) for newly settled "frontier" towns, of which the relatively young community of Wilton was an example. Edward M. Cook, Jr., *The Fathers of the Towns: Leadership and Community Structure in Eighteenth-Century New England* (Baltimore: Johns Hopkins University Press, 1976), pp. 167–69, 181. I have assumed that Wilton would have fit Cook's "Group V" category.

18. Town records excerpted in Livermore and Putnam, *History of Wilton*, p. 72.

19. Ibid., passim.

20. Ibid., p. 55.

21. The baptismal records for 1773 are missing; the figure of seventeen includes only those born in 1773 prior to September 7 who are named in the genealogy section of Livermore and Putnam, *History of Wilton*. It is demonstrable that not all families in town are included in that compilation, so the actual number of such births could easily have been larger than this.

22. Laurel Thatcher Ulrich, *Good Wives: Image and Reality in the Lives of Women in Northern New England, 1650–1750* (New York: Alfred A. Knopf, 1982), pp. 51–52, 126–32.

23. Quoted in Livermore and Putnam, *History of Wilton*, pp. 60–61.

24. David D. Hall, *Worlds of Wonder, Days of Judgment: Popular Religious Belief in Early New England* (Cambridge, Mass.: Harvard University Press, 1989), pp. 15–16.

25. Ulrich, *Good Wives*, pp. 215–16.

26. Livermore and Putnam, *History of Wilton*, p. 318.

27. Church of Christ of Wilton, *The Proceedings and Documents Relative to Certain Members Separating from the Church in Wilton* (Concord, N.H.: Printed by Isaac Hill, 1824), p. 62n.

28. Wilton's population in 1767 was 350. Greene and Harrington, *American Population*, p. 79. For Livermore's additions to the church, see Livermore and Putnam, *History of Wilton*, p. 252.

29. See Cedric R. Cowing, *The Saving Remnant: Religion and the Settling of New England* (Urbana: University of Illinois Press, 1995), pp. 246, 252, for brief discussions of southern and eastern New Hampshire and the Massachusetts North Shore, respectively, as Old Light territory. The exceptions, however, included the minister closest to Wilton in the 1740s, namely the Reverend Daniel Wilkins of Amherst, a New Light. See table, p. 177. Greven describes Andover as "an Old Light non-revivalist town during the 1740s," though many who had migrated to western Massachusetts, Connecticut, and New Hampshire earlier than that became caught up in the revivals in the new communities (*Four Generations*, p. 279). In the 1740s, the main group of Andoverites who settled in Wilton would not yet have left Andover or, for the most part, have yet entered their teens.

30. Abbot, *History of Andover*, p. 104.

31. While there is no direct evidence that the parsonage, now gone, was standing in September 1733, the Livermore and Putnam *History of Wilton* contains a picture of the house with the notation that it was built before 1775 (p. 48). Since Livermore had been on the scene since 1763, it seems highly likely that he was living there at least by 1773, ten years after his settlement.

32. Clifford K. Shipton, *Biographical Sketches of Those Who Attended Harvard College in the Classes 1756–1760 (Sibley's Harvard Graduates*, vol. 14)(Boston: Massachusetts Historical Society, 1968), pp. 550, 648.

33. Shipton makes this assertion in *Sibley's Harvard Graduates*, vol. 14, p. 648. He does not cite his authority for the statement, but it is consistent with my own findings.

34. Wilton Town Records, p. 74.

35. Excerpts from Church and Ministerial Library Minutes (ts., First Church of Wilton), pp. 48, 54. Hereafter cited as Wilton church records.

36. Wilton church records, p. 16.

37. Livermore and Putnam, *History of Wilton*, p. 227.

38. Ibid., p. 114.

39. William J. Gilmore, *Reading Becomes a Necessity of Life: Material and Cultural Life in Rural New England 1780–1785* (Knoxville: University of Tennessee Press, 1989), especially p. 73.

40. See recollections of Abiel Abbot, cited in note 23.

41. See the somewhat speculative treatment of this issue by Philip Greven in *Four Generations*, pp. 279–82.

42. Wilton Town Records, p. 91.

43. Jay Mack Holbrook, *New Hampshire 1776 Census* (Oxford, Mass.: Holbrook Research Institute, 1976), p. 111; Richard F. Upton, *Revolutionary New Hampshire: An Account of the Social and Political Forces Underlying the Transition from Royal Province to American Commonwealth* (Hanover, N.H.: Dartmouth College, 1936. Reprint with new introduction, New York: Octagon Books, 1971), p. 50.

44. For the names of Putnam and Burton, see Livermore and Putnam, *History of Wilton*, p. 197.

Chapter 2. The Meetinghouse

1. Barker is identified as the housewright in charge of the Wilton project in Daniel F. Secomb, *History of the Town of Amherst* (Concord, N.H.: Evans, Sleeper & Woodbury, 1883), p. 493. He would soon be resettling from Stratham, some fifty miles to the east, to Amherst, where he was already involved in another meetinghouse job, and where he would become a deacon of the church.

2. Abiel Livermore and Sewall Putnam, *History of Wilton, Hillsborough County, New Hampshire* (Lowell, Mass.: Marden & Rowell, 1888), p. 134; *Report of Committee of Investigation Appointed by the Citizens of Wilton, To Ascertain the Cause of the Fire by which the Town's Meeting-House was Destroyed* (Boston: Damrell & Moore, 1860).

3. Ronald Jager and Sally Krone, *" . . . A Sacred Deposit": The Meetinghouse in Washington, New Hampshire* (Washington and Portsmouth: Peter E. Randall, 1989).

4. *The History of New Ipswich, From Its First Grant in MCDDXXXVI to the Present Time* (Boston: Gould & Lincoln, 1852), pp. 144–54; Charles Austin Bemis, *History of the Town of Marlborough* (Marlborough: Frost Free Library, 1974; facs. of 1881 ed.), pp. 80–97.

5. Wilton Town Records (ms., New Hampshire State Archives, Concord), p. 60.

6. *History of New Ipswich*, pp. 148, 152. The New Ipswich meetinghouse, raised in 1768, was 60 by 45 by 26 feet. The ground dimensions of other contemporary meetinghouses, with the dates of their raisings, include the following: Londonderry (East Derry), 1769, 65 by 45; Amherst, 1771, 70 by 40; Sandown, 1773, 50 by 46; Temple, 1781, 55 by 42; Washington, 1787, 60 by 45; Mason, 1789, 55 by 45. The Groton meetinghouse, just south of the border in Massachusetts, 65 by 50 by 26 feet, had been raised nearly two decades earlier, in 1754. These dimensions do not include the "porches" attached to some of them, to be discussed in due course.

7. Wilton Town Records, p. 73.

8. Edmund W. Sinnott, *Meetinghouse and Church in Early New England* (New York: McGraw-Hill, 1963), pp. 19–21; Peter Benes and Phillip D. Zimmerman, *New England Meeting House and Church: 1630–1850* (Boston: Boston University and Currier Gallery of Art, 1979), pp. 4–17; Peter Benes, "Twin-Porch versus Single-Porch Stairwells: Two Examples of Cluster Diffusion in Rural Meetinghouse Architecture," *Old-Time New England* 69, nos. 3–4 (Winter-Spring 1979), pp. 1–68; Kevin M. Sweeny, "Meetinghouses, Town Houses, and Churches," *Win-*

terthur Portfolio 28 (Spring 1993), pp. 59–93. Philip Zimmerman's doctoral dissertation, "Ecclesiastical Architecture in the Reformed Tradition in Rockingham County, New Hampshire, 1790–1860" (Boston University, 1984) contains, in chapter 2 (pp. 13–58), a useful discussion of this building type and its background. The form described here persisted in rural areas even while there was a strong movement in the seaports of New England toward classically inspired "church" buildings, following the examples of Christopher Wren and James Gibbs, even among non-Anglican congregations. The First Baptist Meetinghouse of Providence, for example, built in a churchly style inspired directly by Gibbs, was nearly contemporaneous with the Wilton meetinghouse. William H. Pierson, Jr., *American Buildings and Their Architects, Vol. 1: The Colonial and Neoclassical Styles* (New York: Oxford University Press, 1970), pp. 95–98, 137–40.

9. Wilton Town Records, pp. 64–65, 74–76. An alternate reading of the June 3 vote and the physical evidence is that the voters did intend a single porch at the front entrance but that the decision was later in some way rescinded or overridden in favor of the two end-porch design. If so, the two porches need not necessarily have been incorporated in the design at the time of the raising, nor need they necessarily have been built at the same time. The Livermore and Putnam town history of 1888 mentions two porches, one on each end, easily confirmed until recently by the remaining outline of a twelve-by-twelve foot foundation at the west end of the building and the suggestion of a matching one at the east end. It is not clear, however, when the west porch—or for that matter either porch—was added or for how long it remained. It was not authorized at the time of the building's construction, nor is it visible, perhaps only because of the camera angle, in the photograph of the model that appears in the 1888 history. This photograph, however, is very useful for the evidence it supplies that the east porch was later remodeled as a tower and provided with an enclosed belfry at the top. It is clear that this was a nineteenth-century embellishment, since the belfry contains neo-gothic arches and is topped with tiny wooden spires, obviously a product of the early Victorian age. Chances are that these changes were made about 1832, since that was the year the meetinghouse acquired a bell. Livermore and Putnam, *History of Wilton*, p. 130 and plate opposite p. 128.

10. Benes and Zimmerman, *New England Meeting House and Church*, p. 21.

11. Henry Ames Blood, *The History of Temple, N.H.* (Boston: Printed by George C. Band & Avery, 1860), p. 135.

12. Wilton Town Records, pp. 63–64.

13. For two examples of alternate methods, see Jager and Krone, *A Sacred Deposit*, pp. 19–21, and Bemis, *History of Marlborough*, pp. 84–87.

14. Wilton Town Records, pp. 75–76.

15. Lyman S. Hayes, *The Connecticut River Valley in Southern Vermont and New Hampshire* (Rutland, Vt.: The Tuttle Co., 1929), p. 230.

16. The rough estimate of the number of trees that needed to be cut derives from the supposition that the frame required, by my count, about eighty major hewn members such as sills, girders, joists, posts, plates, tie beams, principal rafters, and king posts, each of which required a large, in some cases massive, tree. I have doubled that number to account for what was needed for the many more sawn members such as studs, girts, common rafters, purlins, and braces. This estimate is for the frame alone. It does not include the many more trees that were required for sheathing, clapboards, shingles, and interior finishing. James L. Garvin has found records showing the frame of a three-story urban dwelling built in Dover in 1806 to contain 35,466 board feet. "Academic Architecture and the Building Trades in the Piscataqua Region of New Hampshire and Maine, 1715–1815" (PhD. diss., Boston University, 1983), p. 461.

17. In 1996 the New Hampshire chapter of the Nature Conservancy acquired Sheldrick Forest, a rare long-undisturbed 227-acre tract of old growth pine, hemlock, and hardwoods in the southwest corner of Wilton just south of modern Route 101.

18. James L. Garvin, "The Merciful Restoration of Old Houses" (typescript), pp. 9–12.

19. This assumes six sets of posts, tie beams, and principal rafter assemblies, the usual number for meetinghouses of this date and type. In addition to these six heavy load-bearing posts on each of the long sides of the building, there were probably two "prick posts" that helped support the plate in each end. There would have been two such posts rather than a single centered one in order to allow for a central door on each end. See discussion of prick posts in Abbott Lowell Cummings, *The Framed Houses of Massachusetts Bay, 1625–1725* (Cambridge, Mass.: Harvard University Press, 1979), p. 53.

20. Jager and Krone, *A Sacred Deposit*, pp. 19–21. Abbott Lowell Cummings also discusses the seasonality of cutting in *Framed Houses*, pp. 59–60. One seventeenth-century observer reported that spring cutting was the norm at that time, but admitted that opinions about the best time to cut timber varied widely. He also mentions other much older sources recommending cutting oak in midwinter and in the last quarter of the moon.

21. Eric Sloane, *A Museum of Early American Tools* (New York: Wilfred Funk, Inc., 1964), pp. 48–49. For a quite learned and extensive discussion of the carpenter's tools of the era, many of which had not changed significantly since ancient times, see Henry C. Mercer, *Ancient Carpenters' Tools*, 3d. ed. (Doylestown, Pa.: Bucks County Historical Society, 1960). Whereas Sloane's book and C. Keith Wilbur's *Home Building and Woodworking in Colonial America* (Old Saybrook, Conn.: The

Globe Pequot Presss, 1992) are illustrated with drawings, the Mercer book is illustrated with photographs.

22. There was at least one sawmill in Wilton, owned by Jacob Putnam only a short distance from the common, and probably a second, built by Captain Nathan Hutchinson sometime before the Revolution. Livermore and Putnam, *History of Wilton*, p. 162. For more on the two mills, see note 5 in chapter 6.

23. If the carpenter wanted a smoother surface than he could produce with his broad axe, he could use an adze instead, and even finish it with a plane. This would normally be done, however, only on posts or beams that were intended to be exposed, and it is doubtful that there was much adze or plane work in the Wilton meetinghouse frame except in finishing some of the joints to assure proper fit. Sloan, *Museum of Early American Tools*, pp. 16–17, 26. Garvin, "Merciful Restoration," pp. 13–14.

24. Garvin, "Merciful Restoration," p. 12.

25. Sloan, *Museum of Early American Tools*, pp. 50–51.

26. Sarah Shedd, "All About the Days of the Old Box-Pews" (1859), quoted in Jager and Krone, *A Sacred Deposit*, p. 35.

27. Garvin, "Merciful Restoration," p. 24 and passim; Cummings, *Framed Houses*, see illustrations pp. 56–92. The photographs in fig. 56, p. 60, show several sets of "raising numerals." So does one of Philip Barker's four exceptionally revealing photographs of the interior structure of the Washington meetinghouse (1776) on pp. 30–31 of Jager and Krone, *A Sacred Deposit*. The roof structure of the Washington meetinghouse was essentially identical to the one used in Wilton, consisting of double principal rafters with king post, common rafters distributed between the principals, and horizontal roof boards.

28. "Extract of a letter from New-Ipswich," *Massachusetts Gazette*, September 13, 1773; *Boston Evening-Post*, September 20, 1773; *New Hampshire Gazette*, September 24, 1773; *Connecticut Gazette*, September 28, 1773.

29. The *New Hampshire Gazette* of September 17, 1773, refers to the "middle Beam," which seems to suggest an odd number of posts, beams, king posts, and principals. However, it is extremely unlikely that any meetinghouse of the period would have contained posts in the center of either side of the building, since that would have precluded both a centered front door and the usual treatment of the pulpit and pulpit window on the opposite side. Thus the reference is probably to one of the beams *near* the center, either the third or the fourth from the end, rather than to one in the actual center of the building.

30. See diagram of roof truss consisting of double principals, king post, tie beam, and braces in a meetinghouse (1771) at Farmington, Connecticut, in J. Frederick Kelly, "Raising Connecticut Meeting-Houses," *Old-Time New England* 27 (July, 1936), p. 5.

31. On joists, see Garvin, "Merciful Restoration," p. 15.

32. According to nineteenth-century accounts, this was the method used in Washington in 1787 and in Boscawen (in the section that later became Webster) in 1791. The two accounts, one in verse composed in 1859, the other written in 1878 by a town historian from his father's memory, are remarkably similar in detail. Shedd, "All About the Days of the Old Box-Pews" in Jager and Krone, *A Sacred Deposit*, pp. 34–35; Charles Carleton Coffin, *The History of Boscawen and Webster from 1733 to 1878* (Concord, N.H.: Republican Press Association, 1878), pp. 139–40.

33. Clarke Blair (Fonda, New York) to author, March 7, 1997, and Richard W. Babcock (Williamstown, Massachusetts) to author, March 28, 1997. Both writers, experts on early building techniques, emphasize the use of such devices as an aid to sheer muscle power in raising the frames of buildings with which they are familiar.

34. Several such people have made somewhat convincing arguments that the walls were most likely framed on the floor and raised from the inside, though they do not all agree on specific details. They include Richard W. Babcock (see note 33), a specialist in the preservation, restoration, moving, and rebuilding of eighteenth- and nineteenth-century barns and co-author (with Lauren R. Stevens) of *Old Barns in the New World: Reconstructing History* (Lee, Mass.: Berkshire House Publishers, 1996); Jim Hardy of New Durham, New Hampshire, a professional carpenter with experience erecting modern post-and-beam houses; my brother Llewellyn Clark of Beckett, Massachusetts, a professional engineer and amateur builder who has helped with a barn raising; and my graduate assistant Peter Leavenworth, a building contractor as well as historian in training, with whom I have discussed the Wilton meetinghouse project, including possible raising scenarios, at great length. New Hampshire's official architectural historian James L. Garvin, while stressing that there is no way to know for certain, agrees that what I call the "inside out" scenario makes as much sense as the alternative, if not more. Of the dozens of contemporary sources I have consulted on raising frames of large buildings, nearly all are silent on this detail. However, Sarah Shedd's poem of 1852, on the Washington meetinghouse raising seventy-two years before, describes men gathered at the dormant broadsides "To lift them from the ground" (Jager & Krone, *A Sacred Deposit*, p. 35). In 1936, J. Frederick Kelly speculated that the wall frames of Connecticut meetinghouses "were framed flat on the ground—perhaps in sections" ("Raising Connecticut Meeting-Houses," p. 3). While these two statements cannot but temper one's confidence that the broadsides were framed on the floor and raised outward, neither account rests on eye witness, and in his very cautious and authoritative treatment of his subject, Kelly is careful to acknowledge that on that particular detail, he is guessing. The illustrations in Wilbur, *Home Building and Woodworking in Colonial America* show the bents, or cross sections of a two-story house being raised from the floor, with the aid of gin poles (p. 32). Sev-

eral photographs and diagrams scattered throughout Babcock and Stevens, *Old Barns in the New World*, show the same thing with regard to barns, putting particular emphasis on the use of gin poles, block and tackle, and the "bull wheel," a type of capstan.

35. The ten-by-ten-inch dimensions of the plates are conjectural, but based on detailed plans of the Sandown, New Hampshire, meetinghouse, exactly contemporaneous with Wilton's and of comparable dimensions. The estimated weight assumes the plate was of partly dried pine. An oak beam of the same size, partly dried, would have weighed over a ton.

36. Here is a hearsay account, from memory, of how "General Fuller," a master builder, conducted the raising of the meetinghouse in Rockingham, Vermont, in 1787: "After he got everything ready the old General took a bottle of rum in one hand, a tumbler in the other and stood on the plate of the bent on the south side, then he gave the order to put it up in that position. He rode up on the plate, and he was a man weighing 200 pounds. When they had got it up he stood on the plate, drank his health to the crowd below, then threw his bottle and tumbler down and called for the ladder, coming down amid long and loud cheering." A less detailed account of the same raising states that Fuller "went up with the front broadside, as was customary in those days." Quoted in Hayes, *Connecticut River Valley*, pp. 230–31.

37. The first dialogue is from Coffin, *History of Boscawen*, p. 140. It is based on the recollection of "one of the great events of his boyhood" of the author's father, Thomas Coffin, who was fourteen at the time of the Boscawen raising in 1791 (p. 141). The second is an excerpt from Sarah Shedd's poem quoted in Jager and Krone, *A Sacred Deposit*, p. 35.

38. The *New Hampshire Gazette* of September 17, 1773, reported that the raising was "designed" to be accomplished in nine hours, and that it had been nearly completed by three in the afternoon. The Boscawen raising began "early in the morning," the first broadside was up by nine, and the job finished by noon.

39. Cummings, *Framed Houses*, p. 63.

40. Kelly, "Raising Connecticut Meeting-Houses," pp. 8–9.

41. For a sketch illustrating the use of windlass and "snatch block," see Kelly, "Raising Connecticut Meeting-Houses," p. 8. The possible use of oxen is only a guess, but in a rural community at this time and place there could have been no more obvious source of power if human muscle was not enough.

42. Ephraim Peabody, *An Address, Delivered at the Centennial Celebration in Wilton, N.H., Sept. 25, 1839* (Boston: B. H. Greene, 1839), p. 13.

43. Ibid., p. 11. Peabody states explicitly that the rafters were put up in order from east to west.

44. For a colorful example of the several available accounts of "wet-

ting" the ridgepole, see F. Allen Burt, *The Story of Mount Washington* (Hanover, N.H.: Dartmouth Publications, 1960), p. 257, n. 2, quoted from Benjamin D. Eastman, *North Conway, Its Surroundings, Its Settlement by English People* (North Conway, N.H.: Reporter Press, 1880), pp. 10–11.

Chapter 3. Disaster

1. Daniel F. Secomb, *History of the Town of Amherst, Hillsborough County, New Hampshire* (Concord, N.H.: Evans, Sleeper & Woodbury, 1883), p. 430; D. Donovan and Jacob A. Woodward, *The History of the Town of Lyndeborough, New Hampshire 1735–1905* (Lyndeborough: Published by the Town, 1906), two deeds dated March 22, 1771; and deed dated January 20, 1772, vol. 2, pp. 485, 487.

2. Ephraim Peabody, *An Address, Delivered at the Centennial Celebration in Wilton, N.H., Sept. 25, 1839* (Boston: B. H. Greene, 1839), p. 13. While Peabody reports the coincidence as fact, he does lament that as a result, "Superstition came in to darken the event." Peabody's account is copied in Donovan and Woodward, *History of Lyndeborough*, vol. 1, pp. 147–50.

3. Bradford's visit to the building site and his encounter with Barker are recorded in Peabody's *Address*, pp. 11–12. I have provided conjectural explanations for some of the details of Peabody's narrative. Peabody gave no sources, so it is possible that his account rested on little more than sixty-eight years of folk memory, in which case one must be less confident of their complete accuracy than one would like to be. The exact words attributed to Barker are entirely my own, but they follow those quoted indirectly in Peabody's account: ". . . the master-workman . . . replied to him, that if was afraid he might go home; that they wanted no cowards there" (p. 12). Mrs. Bradford's given name of Sarah is recorded in Daniel Secomb, *History of Amherst*, p. 518.

4. "The Fall of the Wilton (N.H.) Meeting House," *New England Historical and Genealogical Register* 22 (1868), p. 235.

5. Peabody, *Address*, p. 12; "Fall of the Wilton (N.H.) Meeting House," p. 235.

6. For sources and further details on the five fatalities, see chapter 4.

7. *The History of New Ipswich, from Its First Grant in MDCCXXXVI to the Present Time* (Boston: Gould & Lincoln, 1852), p. 69.

8. That it would have taken two days to make a horseback ride to Boston over the most probable seventy-mile route can be inferred from the time it took the Dover minister and historian Jeremy Belknap to ride between Hanover and the White Mountains in the 1770s and 1780s. He averaged thirty-five miles a day. Granted that both terrain and length of journey made the Wilton-to-Boston ride an easier one than Belknap's,

there is small likelihood that a rider would have made the trip without lodging somewhere over one night en route. Donna-Belle Garvin and James L. Garvin, *On the Road North of Boston: New Hampshire Taverns and Turnpikes, 1700–1900* (Concord, N.H.: New Hampshire Historical Society, 1988), pp. 67–68.

9. Lending further strength to the supposition that the letter was written by a clergyman, the writer needed sufficient familiarity with Scripture to provide such a neat combination of two widely separated passages, the first Ecclesiastes 9:12, and the second Matthew 24:44.

10. Though incomplete and containing a few difficult spelling inaccuracies, the *Massachusetts Gazette*'s casualty list compiled in haste by the New Ipswich correspondent provided the starting point in identifying the victims discussed in chapter 4, and serves as the basis for the corrected casualty list in appendix B.

11. *New-Hampshire Gazette*, September 24, 1773. Obviously, it was only domestic news that would have been considered "cold" seventeen days later. The American newspapers of the day, as they had throughout the century, still reported European events that had occurred several months in the past, and news from American provinces remote from their own as much as three or four weeks after the event. The determining factors were transatlantic travel time in the case of European news and, among American cities in this era of mutual copying, publication intervals, travel time by road, and postal schedules.

12. *Massachusetts Gazette and Boston Post-Boy and Advertiser*, September 16 1773.

13. *Connecticut Gazette*, September 17, 1773; *Providence Gazette*, September 18, 1773; *Boston Evening-Post*, September 20, 1773.

14. *Pennsylvania Journal*, September 22, 1773; *New-York Journal or the General Advertiser*, September 23, 1773; *Pennsylvania Gazette*, September 29, 1773. The story did not appear, for example, in either of the two *Virginia Gazettes* of Williamsburg or in the *South Carolina Gazette* of Charleston. There are no readily available files of either of the two North Carolina newspapers, and the extant file of the *South Carolina and American General Gazette* lacks all of the most likely numbers.

Chapter 4. The Victims

1. Unless otherwise indicated, details about the various victims throughout this chapter come from the published town history that is relevant in each case: Abiel Abbot Livermore and Sewall Putnam, *History of the Town of Wilton, Hillsborough County, New Hampshire* (Lowell, Mass.: Marden & Rowell, 1888); D. Donovan and Jacob A. Woodward, *The History of the Town of Lyndeborough, New Hampshire, 1735–1905* (Lyndeborough: Published by the Town, 1906); *The History of*

New Ipswich, from Its First Grant in MDCCXXXVI to the Present Time (Boston: Gould & Lincoln, 1852); Henry Ames Blood, *The History of Temple, N.H.* (Boston: George C. Rand & Avery, 1860.)

2. "Extract of a letter from New-Ipswich," *Massachusetts Gazette*, September 17, 1773 and others, reprinted among other places in Blood, *History of Temple*, pp. 182–83.

3. *History of New Ipswich*, pp. 69, 432, 445.

4. Population figures are from the New Hampshire 1773 census, recorded among other places in Evarts B. Greene and Virginia D. Harrington, *American Population before the Federal Census of 1790* (New York: Columbia University Press, 1932; repr. Gloucester, Mass.: Peter Smith, 1966), pp. 74–79. For Lyndeborough, the census reported only "polls" (white males over the age of twenty-one), who numbered 108. I have applied Greene's and Harrington's standard factor of four to arrive at a conjectured whole population of 432. For the other towns mentioned here, the census recorded both polls and "inhabitants."

5. For the complete casualty list, see appendix B. The core source is the list appended to "Extract of a letter from New-Ipswich," which contains the names of forty-three persons, a few of them so badly spelled as to require considerable search in other sources to determine who was most likely meant. The forty-three included one Wilton victim whose first name was Benjamin but whose surname was omitted. If that name was either reported by mistake or is actually the wrong identification of someone else on the list, the *Gazette's* list is then reduced to forty-two. The casualties omitted from the newspaper report were largely from Lyndeborough, but Donovan's and Woodward's *History of Lyndeborough* contains a complete casualty list for that town (vol. 1, p. 149), making it possible to add nine additional names. The fifty-second and fifty-third names are those of William Spear of New Ipswich and Isaac Brewer of Temple. *The History of New Ipswich* provides Spear's name along with the correct spelling (Wright) for the "Simeon Rite" of the *Gazette's* list (pp. 249, 445). Brewer's name is found on the list of six Temple casualties (rather than the five in the newspaper report) in Blood, *History of Temple*, p. 183. If the resulting list is correct, we are still left with the mystery of "Benjamin———" of Wilton and the possibility that there may have been a fifty-fourth victim as well, though the ballad and other sources that are specific about numbers use the figure of fifty-three. The few remaining ambiguities as to exact identity, usually involving relatives with the same name, are indicated in the appendix.

6. Although it is possible that Archelaus had already married Mary Nichols in 1773, it seems much more likely that his marriage was at least two years in the future, since Jacob deeded part of the farm to him in 1776 shortly before the birth of his and Mary's first son. He got the rest of the farm by bequest upon Jacob's death in 1781. Livermore and Putnam, *History of Wilton*, p. 477.

7. Though it seems to me beyond much question that the Alexander Milliken (or Miliken or Mullikan) on the casualty list was Samuel's brother, there is nothing in the record to prove that it may not instead have been Alexander, Sr., whose age in 1773 is not known.

8. *New England Historical and Genealogical Register* 121 (1967), p. 143.

9. Unless Lyndeborough's Jonathan Chamberlain who appears on the casualty list was the senior Jonathan Chamberlain, sixty-three, rather than the twenty-nine-year-old Jonathan, Jr., as I have assumed despite the index entry in *History of New Ipswich*, which could be taken to indicate that the victim was the older man.

10. Ages in every case are determined from the genealogical sections of the town histories of the four communities except in the case of Simeon Fletcher, whose birth and death dates are recorded in *NEHGR* 121 (1967), p. 143. The average age of twenty-nine does not take account of Ephraim Barker, the master builder, who was from outside the vicinity and in any case could be presumed because of his experience to be older than most of the building crew. He was forty-one.

11. New Ipswich tax information is based on an analysis of the tables in *History of New Ipswich*, pp. 70–71. On Reuben Kidder, see ibid., pp. 408–12. Going on the (possibly erroneous) assumption that Elizabeth Kidder Livermore was born in 1743 and married for the first time in 1765 to Zacheus Greene of Concord, Massachusetts, we surmise that she was the daughter of Thomas Kidder, a brother of Reuben Kidder. Livermore and Elizabeth were married in 1769. F. E. Kidder, *A History of the Kidder Family* (Allston, Mass.: F. E. Kidder, 1886), pp. 25–26; Walter Eliot Thwing, *The Livermore Family of America* (Boston: W.B. Clarke Co., 1902), p. 80.

12. *History of New Ipswich*, p. 143n.

13. Ibid., p. 437; the will of Joseph Tucker's father Moses is in *State Papers of New Hampshire*, 39 (1941), pp. 207–10.

14. *History of New Ipswich* contains little specific information on Fletcher's family. The identity of his wife is assumed from the presence on the 1774 town tax list of "Widow Rachel Fletcher," assessed at a substantial one pound, seven shillings, sixpence, placing her close to the upper quarter of the town's taxpayers. The presence of children in the family, probably more than one, since Fletcher was thirty-six at the time of his death, is easily inferred from the *History's* entry (p. 374) noting "descendants" of Fletcher in New Ipswich in 1852.

15. Although the ages of the Carlton brothers are not precisely known, both were obviously rather young men, since they were the fifth and sixth children respectively of Jeremiah and Eunice and both apparently still unmarried and probably living at home, though it also appears that David Carlton owned some land on his own account as early as 1770

(Donovan and Woodward, *History of Lyndeborough*, p. 486). For reference to David as a Bunker Hill casualty, see ibid., p. 151.

16. *State Papers of New Hampshire* 30 (1910), pp. 3–4, 159–61.

17. Livermore and Putnam, *History of Wilton*, p. 87.

18. Ibid., pp. 88–89.

19. Ibid., pp. 93, 100.

20. These totals, which are no doubt incomplete, are compiled from the relevant town histories with some reference to rolls in *State Papers of New Hampshire*. For Chandler, see Sarah Loring Bailey, *Historical Sketches of Andover* (Boston: Houghton, Mifflin, 1880), pp. 344–45.

Chapter 5. The Ballad

1. *A FUNERAL ELEGY, occasioned by the TRAGEDY At Salem, near Boston, on Thursday Afternoon, the 17th of June, 1773* (Bds., [Salem, 1773]). One cannot help thinking of Franklin's hilarious (and unkind) Dogood No. 7, "A Receipt to make a New-England Funeral Elegy," first published in the *New-England Courant*, June 25, 1722.

2. Isaiah Thomas, *The History of Printing in America*, edited by Marcus A. McCorison (Barre, Mass.: Imprint Society, 1970), pp. 176–77.

3. Ephraim Peabody, *An Address, Delivered at the Centennial Celebration in Milton, N.H., September 25, 1839*, p. 13n; *The History of New Ipswich, from its First Grant in MDCXXXVI to the Present Time* (Boston: Gould & Lincoln, 1852), p. 69.

4. For a discussion of possibilities, see appendix D.

5. The attribution to Nathaniel Allen is in *New England Historical and Genealogical Register* 22 (1868), pp. 234–35, and in an appendix of Edward Fletcher, *Descendants of Robert Fletcher* (Boston: Rand, Avery & Co., 1881), p. 528. Asa Black is the name on the title page of the manuscript, dated 1773, once owned by Clarke Blair of Fonda, New York. However, this is the only copy I have seen, published or unpublished, that dates the accident erroneously—September 17 instead of September 7. The third possibility, the Massachusetts schoolteacher, derives from a reference to another manuscript copy in Abiel Livermore and Sewall Putnam, *History of the Town of Wilton, Hillsborough County, New Hampshire* (Lowell, Mass.: Marden & Rowell, 1888), p. 131: "In giving this poem we follow a copy, found by a resident of Topsham, Vermont, among the papers of his father, who received it, when a boy in Massachusetts, from his teacher, a one-legged man, name unknown, who is supposed to have been the author." I have been unable to identify either Allen or Black. The Polly Lewis-Phebe Howard copy of the ballad, while shedding no light on the identity of the author, does contain a suggestion, by no means conclusive, that the ballad was actually composed in

Wilton soon after the event. At the end of the poem, in the copyist's hand, appears "Finis," followed by a short series of decorative marks, and then "Wilton September 1773," as if the place and date were part of the copied text.

6. The copy in my possession, marked "Polly Lewis her Verses" and dated May 1779 (two months before she apparently presented it as gift to my infant ancestor Phebe Howard), seems to have been prepared as a project in penmanship.

7. G. Malcolm Laws, Jr., *Native American Balladry*, rev. ed. (Philadelphia: American Folklore Society, 1964), p. 9.

8. Tristram P. Coffin, introduction to 1966 edition of Helen Hartness Flanders et al., *The New Green Mountain Songster: Traditional Folk Songs of Vermont* (Hartboro, Penn.: Folklore Associates, Inc., 1966), pp. ix–x.

9. For a definition and discussion of "publication" in the scribal medium, applied in this instance to seventeenth-century England and to much more purposeful, even professional practices than was the case here, see Harold Love, *Scribal Publication in Seventeenth-Century England* (Oxford: Clarendon Press, 1993), pp. 35–46.

10. On the "preservative powers of print," including "typographical fixity," see Elizabeth Eisenstein, *The Printing Revolution in Early Modern Europe* (Cambridge: Cambridge University Press, 1983), pp. 78–88. This convenient volume, accessible to the general reader but lacking scholarly apparatus except for a fairly extensive list of selected readings, is an attractively illustrated abridgment of the author's full-scale *The Printing Press as an Agent of Change*, 2 vols. (Cambridge: Cambridge University Press, 1979).

11. Derived from my own measurement of the half sheet upon which the earliest *Boston News-Letter* was printed, and which Isaiah Thomas called "pot"—as distinct from several larger categories such as "crown" and "foolscap." See Charles E. Clark, *The Public Prints: The Newspaper in Anglo-American Culture, 1660–1740* (New York: Oxford University Press, 1994), p. 84; Thomas, *History of Printing in America*, p. 215.

12. As a proud grandparent, I have been watching with fascination a recent trend in elementary education that encourages writing and inspires creativity by making "published" authors of schoolchildren. "Publication," a term deliberately and far from inaccurately used in the classroom, consists of producing a student's story or other piece of writing in a booklike pamphlet, often illustrated and designed for at least some degree of permanence. (Instead of being packed away in a box of "schoolwork" in the attic, it can be displayed with other publications on a bookshelf.) Although there is usually only one copy of each "publication," it is produced in a professional-seeming form that not only creates a pride of ownership but also can be shared with a multiple readership, namely

classmates and family members. This practice seems to me a modern adaptation of what these two copyists of the ballad intended to accomplish.

13. This broadside appears in none of the standard bibliographies, nor is there a copy in the extensive broadside collection of the American Antiquarian Society. I have seen only a photocopy, held by the Wilton Historical Society, of an original whose whereabouts are unknown. The document itself is undated, but the fire occurred on November 3, 1818, and since the broadside reports it as news, it must have been printed shortly thereafter. A brief colophon on the reverse side reads "Printed for N. Coverly, Milk Street." The younger Coverly was in business on his own in Milk Street, Boston, from 1810 until about 1823. Worthington Chauncey Ford, "The Isaiah Thomas Collection," *American Antiquarian Society Proceedings* 33 (1923), p. 53. Of course it is possible that the ballad was simply printed on the back of the remaining copies of the news broadside, in which case it would have been printed later than 1818, or the reverse, in which case it could have been printed earlier. Obviously, however, these two accounts of local tragedies were linked in the printer's mind, and it seems likely that he perceived the Boston fire as an occasion that might stimulate interest in the Wilton event forty-three years earlier.

14. Ford, "The Isaiah Thomas Collection," p. 52.

15. Peabody, *An Address*, pp. 64–66; *History of New Ipswich*, p. 69n (six stanzas only); *NEHGR* 22 (1868), pp. 234–35; Fletcher, *Descendants*, p. 528 (six stanzas only); Livermore and Putnam, *History of Wilton* pp. 131–32. The one twentieth-century printing is copied from the manuscript owned by Clarke Blair. It appears at the end of an article summarizing Mr. Peabody's account of the tragedy in his 1839 centennial address under the title "All in a Suden, a Beme Broke!" in *Yankee* 34, no. 9 (September, 1970), pp. 98, 100–101, 156–60. The ten stanzas extracted from the Blair copy are on p. 160.

16. Laws, *Native American Balladry*, p. 1. One could debate at length about what constitutes a "folksong." At one point in his discussion, Laws seems to suggest that oral transmission is the essential quality; that looser sense qualifies the Wilton verses as a "folksong" and makes it possible to apply to our example his more refined definition of a ballad, namely "a narrative folksong which dramatizes a memorable event."

17. For example, Worthington Chauncy Ford, *Broadsides, Ballads, &c. Printed in Massachusetts 1639–1800*, Vol. 25 of Massachusetts Historical Society *Collections* (Boston, 1922), supplemented by Ford, "The Isaiah Thomas Collection of Ballads," pp. 34–112.

18. Printed, probably for the first time, in Henry Ames Blood, *The History of Temple, N.H.* (Boston: George C. Rand & Avery, 1860), pp. 179–82.

19. Ford, "The Isaiah Thomas Collection," p. 34.

20. See discussion of ballad forms in Laws, *Native American Balladry*, pp.68–70.

21. My colleague David Watters suggests that the verses are "stitched together" from three generic sources, the ballad, the elegy, and the sermon, with an undercurrent of hymn singing. For consistency's sake, I have used a single source, the Polly Lewis-Phebe Howard copy, for the quotations from the ballad in the text that follows here and in the epigraphs at the head of each chapter. A transcript of that copy appears with two other versions in Appendix C. I have tried to be scrupulousy accurate in transcribing, but there are difficulties with the manuscript that I probably have not surmounted. In particular, the copyist did a poor job of distinguishing between the upper and lower case "S," and often the "G" as well, as an initial letter. That copy, the reader may notice, is virtually unpunctuated.

22. These examples are all taken from the list of first lines in Ford, "The Isaiah Thomas Collection," pp. 103–111.

23. Laws, *Native American Balladry*, p. 226, quoting from Helen Creighton, *Maritime Folk Songs* (Toronto: Ryerson Press, 1962), p. 208.

24. *History of New Ipswich*, p. 69.

25. In the famous *Sinners in the Hands of an Angry God* (1741).

26. See chapter 1.

Chapter 6. After the Fall

1. See again chapter 3. The reference to "Old Boston," as his townsmen called him, is in *History of New Ipswich, from Its First Grant in MDCCXXXVI to the Present Time* (Boston: Gould & Lincoln, 1852) p. 257, that to Caesar's story-telling in "Fall of the Wilton Meeting House," *New England Historical and Genealogical Register* 22 (1868), 235.

2. September 16, 1773. See chapter 3.

3. The assumption that the Wilton fast was on one of these Thursdays follows from the fact that Thursday was invariably the day of the week upon which New Englanders held days of fasting and humiliation or of thanksgiving in response to specific acts of divine intrusion, as the founders believed, into human affairs. Possibly that was because Thursday had customarily been the day of the weekly lecture in Boston. The custom survives in rudimentary form in the modern annual Thanksgiving day, a Thursday, which in New Hampshire was balanced until recently by a fixed annual fast day at the opposite side of the calendar. Until 1949, when that observance was shifted to a Monday, New Hampshire's Fast Day was held on the last Thursday in April. It was abandoned altogether in 1991.

4. Thomas Beede, "A Topographical and Historical Description of

Wilton, N.H.," *Farmer's and Moore's Historical Collections of New Hampshire* I (June 1, 1822), 68.

5. Abiel Livermore and Sewall Putnam, *History of the Town of Wilton, Hillsborough County, New Hampshire* (Lowell, Mass.: Marden & Rowell, 1888) p. 162. Another sawmill, combined with gristmill, was built before the Revolution by Captain Nathan Hutchinson, but it is not clear whether this mill, in addition to Putnam's, was available in 1773. If it was, the boards for the meetinghouse could have come from there instead or as well, though transportation to the building site, involving a trip of several uphill miles, would have been more difficult than from Putnam's conveniently located mill. There is no surviving record of whether it was Putnam or Hutchinson, or both, who submitted the winning bid, but at this distance it seems likely that Putnam would have been better situated to do the job more cheaply.

6. Although it is certain that the meetinghouse had both an east and a west porch at some time in its history, it is not clear whether the east porch is the one authorized to be built on the "foreside" (Wilton Town Records [ms., New Hampshire State Archives, Concord], p. 76) and therefore built at the same time as the main building. See chapter 2, note 9.

7. According to James Garvin, skiving and lapping was almost universal in New England until well into the nineteenth century. See his discussion of this and other building techniques in "The Merciful Restoration of Old Houses" (ts), pp. 46–48.

8. Wilton Town Records, pp. 77, 83–85. The "school money" was a separate appropriation funded by a distinct tax levy. At that point in the year, some of the school fund had been collected and loaned out at interest and some was still owed by taxpayers, who were now given until the following October to pay.

9. Wilton Town Records, p. 83. For a comparable approach to selling pews in 1787, see Ronald Jager and Sally Krone, ". . . *A Sacred Deposit*": *the Meetinghouse in Washington, New Hampshire* (Washington and Portsmouth: Peter E. Randall, 1989), pp. 22–25. Ola E. Winslow describes the older method of assigning pews "according to dignity, age, estate, and 'whatever else tends to make a man respectable'" in *Meetinghouse Hill, 1630–1763* (New York: Macmillan, 1952), pp. 142–49.

10. Wilton Town Records, p. 91. The record actually names a John Abbott to the committee to finish the inside instead of Jacob Abbott. However, the extensive Abbott family genealogy in Livermore and Putnam, *History of Wilton*, shows no John Abbott of the right age and generation in any branch of the family. It seems likely that the voters decided to keep the committee elected just two months earlier intact, and that a mistake was made in the recording. At this point, the selectmen were still pursuing the matter of porches, having been rebuffed by the voters on this point several times. Somewhat mysteriously, since one

porch on the "foreside" had already been approved the previous June and possibly framed at the raising, the voters "negatived" a warrant item to see about building "porches."

11. Wilton Town Records, pp. 102, 107. The town voted its response to the two men's requests on March 13.

12. For example, in the well preserved Sandown, New Hampshire, meetinghouse, built in 1773, the same year as Wilton's.

13. Wilton Town Records, pp. 91, 98–99; the record of the auction of rights to the long pews, held at Richard Taylor's tavern on January 3, 1775, is in the Wilton Town Records, p. 156. All rights are designated "men's side" or "women's side."

14. Livermore and Putnam mention the pulpit and sounding board in *History of Wilton*, p. 130, but are skimpy on details.

15. This was the standard layout of the period, from which rural New England meetinghouses never deviated. James Garvin, New Hampshire's official architectural historian, has even observed that country meetinghouses at least in that province seem invariably to have been oriented to the compass in the same way, with the broad front side toward the south and the pulpit on the north side. If this is indeed the case, there are several possible explanations. We might speculate, recalling that the meetinghouses of the period were always unheated, that it was reasoned that since the pulpit side would always have been the one side lacking a door, that wall would provide somewhat better protection than any of the alternatives from the winter north wind. Another, less likely possibility is that this orientation offered the preferred direction of sunlight. Yet another is the earliest builders' subtle, possibly subconscious modification of the Anglican practice of orienting the long axis of churches east and west, with the altar end invariably in the east. Meetinghouses with their broad sides facing north and south would retain an east-west orientation of the long axis even though the focus of worship was directed across the breadth of the building rather than along its length and therefore, perhaps in part because it seemed one more explicit rejection of the liturgical practices of the past, north rather than east. This generalization does not apply to more heavily built-up areas, where space considerations may have dictated a different orientation. The long axis of the Portsmouth North Meetinghouse of 1712, for example, was north-south with the main entrance on the east side and the pulpit presumably against the west wall.

16. Salma Hale, "Annals of the Town of Keene, From its First Settlement, in 1734, to the year 1790," New Hampshire Historical Society *Collections* 2 (1827), pp. 80–85. For another vote directing "workmanlike" construction of a meetinghouse (in 1768), see Caleb Butler, *History of the Town of Groton, including Pepperrell and Shirley* (Boston: Press of T. R. Marvin, 1848), p. 311.

17. Wilton Town Records, pp. 102, 115, 129. The old meetinghouse

was sold at an auction supervised by Selectman Richard Taylor, the materials hauled away by the unnamed purchaser.

18. See chapter 5.

19. The Reverend Thomas Beede's "Topographical and Historical Description of Wilton. N.H." in *Farmer's and Moore's Historical Collections of New Hampshire* 1 (June 1, 1882), pp. 66–72, the only source I've seen for the fast day, gives the wrong citation with the quotation: Isaiah 127.1, which does not exist. The actual location of the text is Psalm 127.1.

20. I Chronicles 29.14.

21. Jonathan Livermore and Abiel Abbot Livermore, *Two Dedication Sermons, Delivered in Wilton, N.H., Before the First Congregational Church and Society in That Town* (New York: John A. Gray, 1861), p. 1.

22. "Meetinghouse" and "church," of course, are architectural as well as ecclesiastical terms. As applied to an architectural form, a "meetinghouse" is oriented, like Wilton's, across the width of the building; a "church" is oriented longitudinally, the main entrance at one narrow end, the altar and pulpit at the other. During the transition stage in the nineteenth century, this important shift in religious terminology did not always coincide precisely with correct architectural language.

23. For an earlier adoption of non-Puritan ideas about sacred space by Congregationalists in Portsmouth, in this case probably under the influence of a competing Anglican congregation, see Charles E. Clark, *The Eastern Frontier: The Settlement of Northern New England 1610–1763* (New York: Alfred A. Knopf, 1970), p. 298. Richard L. Bushman offers an interesting analysis of Anglican influences on New England ecclesiastical architecture and practices in *The Refinement of America: Persons, Houses, Cities* (New York: Alfred A. Knopf, 1992), pp. 169–80.

24. Livermore and Livermore, *Two Dedication Sermons*, p. 16.

25. Ibid., p. 17.

26. Ibid.

27. Ibid., p. 21.

28. Ibid., pp. 20–21.

29. Stephen Nissenbaum, *The Battle for Christmas* (New York: Alfred A. Knopf, 1996).

30. Livermore and Putnam, *History of Wilton*, pp. 252–53. Clifford K. Shipton makes the same assumption in *Biographical Sketches of Those Who Attended Harvard College in the Classes of 1756–1760 (Sibley's Harvard Graduates,* vol. 14) (Boston: Massachusetts Historical Society, 1968), pp. 648–49.

Index

The names of the accident victims are in **bold type**.

UNIVERSITY PRESS OF NEW ENGLAND publishes books under its own imprint and is the publisher for Brandeis University Press, Dartmouth College, Middlebury College Press, University of New Hampshire, Tufts University, and Wesleyan University Press.

Library of Congress Cataloging-in-Publication Data
Clark, Charles E., 1929–
    The meetinghouse tragedy : an episode in the life of a New England town / Charles E. Clark; including illustrations by John W. Hatch.
        p.   cm.
    Includes bibliographical references (p.   ).
    ISBN 0–87451–887–3 (cloth : alk. paper). — ISBN 0–87451–872–5 (pbk. : alk. paper)
        1. Wilton (N.H. : Town)—History—18th century. 2. Church buildings—New Hampshire—Wilton (Town)—History—18th century. 3. Building—Accidents—New Hampshire—Wilton (Town)—History—18th century. I. Title.
F44.W6C58   1998
974.2'8—dc21   98–23577